RECONNECTING

*How to Renew
and Preserve the 3 Vital
Elements of a Powerful
Spiritual Life*

RONNIE W. FLOYD

BROADMAN & HOLMAN PUBLISHERS
Nashville, Tennessee

© Copyright 1993

Broadman & Holman Publishers

All rights reserved

4260-88
ISBN: 0-8054-6088-8

Dewey Decimal Classification: 248.4
Subject Heading: CHRISTIAN LIFE
Library of Congress Card Catalog Number:
Printed in the United States of America

Unless otherwise stated, all Scripture quotations are from the
Holy Bible, *New American Standard Bible*, copyright © The Lockman
Foundation, 1960, 1962, 1963, 1968, 1971, 1972, 1973, 1975, 1977.
Used by permission.

Library of Congress Cataloging-in-Publication Data

Floyd, Ronnie W., 1955-
    Reconnecting : How to renew and preserve the 3 vital
elements of a powerful spiritual life / by Ronnie Floyd.
    p. cm.
ISBN 0-8054-6088-8
1. Spiritual life—Christianity. I. Title.
BV4501.2.F574 1993
248.4—dc20
                                                    93-11191
                                                      CIP

I WOULD LIKE TO DEDI-
cate this book to my wife, Jeana, who was used as an instrument
of God through her triumph over cancer, so that each of us will
never forget the power of reconnecting with God.

Acknowledgments

THIS BOOK COULD NEVER have been accomplished without the assistance and support of many wonderful people. Above all, I want to thank God for His blessed Holy Spirit that prompted me to write it. He answered my prayer for clarity of thought and the passion to relate the principles found in these pages.

I want to thank Chuck Wilson, president of Broadman and Holman Publishers, for believing in me as a person with a message to share with the world. Thank you, Mike Hyatt, for your encouragement, counsel, and patience with me. Thank you, Jimmy Draper, for having a dream and making the commitment to make Broadman and Holman Publishers a world-class publishing house.

Without Dollie Havens, my administrative assistant, this book would not have been possible. I cannot forget her endless hours of helping me in the details of the manuscript. Thank you, Dollie, for all your help.

On many occasions, I "bounced" a myriad of ideas off my wife, Jeana. She often stopped whatever she was doing to listen to me. Thanks, Jeana, for helping me in this area of preparation and for encouraging me along the way.

Thank you, Josh and Nicholas, my two sons, for giving up some time we could have spent together and sharing your Daddy with others through the writing of this book. It is my prayer that you will live your lives understanding that the contents of this book will lead you to the ultimate success in each of your lives.

Contents

Introduction

UNCERTAINTIES ABOUND in the lives of people today. The only constant thing in our world is change. Nothing stays the same. The fast pace of society only adds to this feeling of uncertainty. As each of our lives are cluttered with our culture's influence, we wonder if there is any power for us to embrace during these changing times.

Few Christians have spiritual power as their first goal in life. Communication with God is limited; therefore, spiritual power is low. Our ever-changing society distracts and interrupts our lives so much that the goal of most Christians is simple survival, a humanistic nature. The results of this mentality are disorderly and chaotic lives that operate from crisis to crisis, rather than lives that are filled with purpose and joy.

I wrote this book to motivate you to reconnect with God. In addition, I want to provide you with practical assistance which can help you live an orderly, balanced, and powerful spiritual life.

Are you ready to change your goal from survival to spiritual power? Are you ready to learn the three vital elements of a powerful spiritual life? This book is for everyone. Take the challenge of disciplining yourself to reading and implementing its contents. The result will be spiritual power.

The Problem and the Answer

Wherever I go I hear Christians saying, "We're tired." As I evaluate their lives and schedules with them, I sense that they are experiencing much frustration. The rat race of our ever-changing society has put them under heavy stress.

I always attempt to bring God into the conversation to determine where He fits into their lives. As I talk with them about their walk with Christ, I learn that it is sporadic and very frustrating. I ask them about their personal devotional life and I immediately sense their guilt. Typically, they describe the many times they have tried to have a personal walk with Jesus but always become distracted and interrupted by life's activities.

The problem is not our ever-changing society. The problem is not the horrendous schedules we all face. The problem is not even the interruptions or distractions we are all conscious of as we attempt to walk with Christ. The problem is a lack of spiritual power, which results in a life of chaos and disorder. The problem is that we are not reconnecting daily with God. This is the only answer each of us has.

Throughout this book I am going to open up my life to you. You will see of many great disappointments I have faced, as well as some very difficult challenges my entire family has had to endure and overcome. This book comprises my life message. You will see when and how I learned valuable spiritual principles. Perhaps through what God has taught me, He can teach you some practical helps to reconnect with Him. I have written this book as the result of my passion to share with you how you can possess spiritual power.

The Big Picture

I realize that most Christians I know desire to walk in spiritual power and victory. Even though many have failed miserably in their efforts, I believe that the seed of God's Spirit lives in them and that they deeply desire to walk in His power. If you have proclaimed, "I do not know how to walk in spiritual power, " do not give up. I do not presume to know everything there is to know about reconnecting with God, but I am excited about all that God is teaching me in my own life.

In part 1, "The Upward Connection," we see that, even though we periodically drift away from God, we have a God who desires to reconnect with us. As we discover God's gracious gesture of desiring to fellowship with us, I provide practical steps every believer can take to reconnect with Him.

In part 2, "The Inward Connection," we find that as we reconnect with God we become aware of our sinfulness and how we can have our passion for God renewed daily. Through this experience, we discover who we are in Christ. This portion of the book closes by challenging every person to be radical in their desire to reconnect with God.

In part 3, "The Outward Connection," we see the essentials of having priorities that will lead us to a life of order and prepare us for life's real issues.

My Dreams for This Book

For some time I have prayed daily for God to give me the opportunity to make a difference in believers' lives. To this end I have dreamed of writing a book that would relate my heart to Christians everywhere. As I have prayed and fasted, asking God for a word to share, He has etched it deeply into my own life, enabling me to share this word with others.

My first dream for *Reconnecting* is that believers will be motivated and encouraged to discipline themselves to walk with Christ. While walking with Christ is never easy, it is always rewarding. I would consider this book to be successful if just one believer becomes radical for God because of renewed motivation to reconnect with Him.

My second dream for Reconnecting is that it might contribute to the needed spiritual awakening in America and across our world. Spiritual awakening also is needed in the church today. This will be possible, though, only when individual believers daily reconnect with God. Then their lives will testify to others of Christ's power as they live orderly, balanced, and powerful spiritual lives. My prayer every day is, "Lord, give America and our world spiritual awakening in my lifetime."

My third dream for *Reconnecting* is that Sunday School classes, discipleship groups, small Bible study groups, and even accountability groups will use this book as a tool for study and instruction. Its contents, when obeyed, have the power to radically change the lives of all Christians.

My final and most important dream for *Reconnecting* is that God will anoint it powerfully as each person reads it. I pray that every believer will be drawn continually to its pages until completed.

May you be driven to read *Reconnecting* and let the Lord use it in your life to motivate and encourage you to order, balance, and spiritual power through daily reconnection with God.

Part One

The
Upward
Connection

1

The
Drift
Factor

FOR SEVERAL MONTHS, I had felt like I was living in a whirlwind. I sensed that I had little control over my own destiny. People around me had unintentionally placed unrealistic expectations on my life. Due to my desire for approval and recognition from my peers, I suffered one of the greatest disappointments in my life.

While driving back from Little Rock, Arkansas, on this cold fall afternoon, I became aware of so many things that had been taking place in my life. I was living on such a fast track that life had gotten out of focus. I was young and somewhat successful, but this time my success greeted me as an enemy, not as a friend. I was obsessed with how I was going to survive this disappointment.

My intentions had been good. I was still spending time with God consistently. However, something was wrong. I had become a victim of my own pride. I had become so consumed with my desire for success that I had drifted away from God. I felt disconnected from Him, and not until now, this very moment, had I even been aware of it.

In the previous month I had begun to hear God's wake-up call to me. I knew the direction I was heading was not where I needed to go, but it seemed like there was no way for me to get off this merry-go-round of life. In these moments, I felt empty and did not know why.

The reason for my emptiness was that I had drifted away from God.

Is it possible to have a daily time with God and still drift away from Him? Is it possible to be active doing the things of God and, while serving, drift away from Him? Is it possible to stand for truth and, while standing, drift away from God? These questions were surging from the depths of my soul. At the time, my answer to these questions was no. In time, my answer changed to yes. The very things I had warned my congregation about had trapped me.

The drift factor occurs when a person is disconnected from God and does not even know it. Drifting away from God never begins with anger toward Him. It never begins with a person shaking his fist toward heaven. The drift factor occurs so slowly in our spiritual life that most people are not even aware of it. It surfaces gradually as one's life loses its focus, becomes disordered, and ultimately loses its spiritual power. When a person's primary goal in life becomes mere survival of a schedule or circumstances, rather than spiritual power, then that person is a victim of the drift factor.

In these busy times it is easy to drift away from God. Even though God never moves away because of His grace commitment to us, at times we move away from Him. We do not do this intentionally, but it happens. The drift factor can happen to anyone. It could be the greatest mountain we must conquer in our Christian life.

The Disposition We Share

Years ago I pastored a church located in a small fishing community on the Gulf Coast of Texas. One of my most pleasant memories of living in that area is of the frequent drives I took along the beautiful seashore. Jeana, my wife, would join me on many late afternoons just to cruise along the roadway that followed the water's edge. The water seemed to have no end as we looked toward the Gulf. Yet this great span of water served as the home of many shrimp boats that came to dock late in the afternoon.

While I enjoyed living near the Gulf and seeing its beauty, I had a tremendous respect for the water. I saw it as a mystery and often wondered what was beneath the surface of the waves. I am not an avid fisherman. However, while I lived in this fishing community there were many times when I went fishing with friends because I was so drawn to the water. Due to my fear of the water, I immediately fastened a life jacket securely around my body every time I went out in a boat. In fact, the joke around the church was that I was the only preacher my congregation had ever had who wore a life jacket in the baptistry.

On one occasion I remember going fishing with a friend named Buddy. As we returned to the dock, Buddy yelled for me to tie the boat's rope to a post on the dock. The water was calm, and I tied the rope to the best of my ability. I then scurried around, helping Buddy gather the gear we would take off the boat. As I turned around and started to step over the side of the boat, I realized we were at least 20 feet from the dock. I was one step away from trying to walk on the water. My leg froze in midair, and I was suddenly aware that I had not tied the rope securely. Buddy laughed. Once again he started the boat's motor and guided us to the dock. This time he decided that he would fasten the rope.

I learned a lot by going fishing during those years, but the greatest lesson I learned was how quickly a boat could drift without my realizing it. Even when the water was calm, the boat would drift in a very subtle manner. At one moment I thought I was one step from the landing, and a moment later I was surprised to see that the boat was far from the dock.

The disposition we share is that at times we all drift from God without even knowing it. Every person can fall prey to the times in which we live. If we are not careful, we will become victims of our circumstances. Our disposition toward drifting is the common denominator that we all share. This tendency can cause us to abandon the goal of living a life connected with God.

Much is being written about the Baby Boomers and Baby Busters in our society. The Baby Boomer generation was born between 1946 and 1964. These are people with high expectations and who have different values than the generation before them. Baby Boomers are continually in search of things that will give meaning to life. Baby Busters are people who were born after 1964. This generation lives only for today. Their life is usually fast-paced and somewhat unfocused. The Baby Buster generation delays their adolescence to enjoy their self-centeredness a little longer. Needless to say, these two groups are seeking real meaning in life, even though they are going about it in various ways. None of us should be surprised at this because every generation before them was seeking the same thing: real meaning in life.

Baby Boomers have much in common with the children of Israel who lived in Old Testament times. As the people of God saw Him deliver them from Egypt, roll back the Red Sea, and supply them with food in the middle of the wilderness, their expectations increased. They wandered aimlessly for 40 years. One moment they were seeing Moses come down the mountain with the Ten Commandments in his hands; the next moment they were making a golden calf to worship. Self-gratification seemed to rule their every step. Even though they were so close to God, even God's chosen people, they possessed the tendency to drift away from Him. They experienced the reality of the drift factor. At times they were disconnected from God and did not even know it.

When Jesus walked upon the earth, He particularly enjoyed the fellowship of Lazarus, Mary, and Martha. It was in their home that He felt comfortable. As Martha welcomed Jesus to her home, the Bible gives us the following insight in Luke 10:39-42:

And she had a sister called Mary, who moreover was listening to the Lord's word, seated at His feet. But Martha was distracted with all her preparations; and she came up to Him, and said, "Lord, do You not care that my sister has left me to do all the serving alone? Then tell her to help me." But the Lord answered and said to her, "Martha, Martha, you are worried and bothered about so many things; but only a few things are necessary, really only one, for Mary has chosen the good part, which shall not be taken away from her."

Martha's characteristics in this passage are very similar to the characteristics of our Baby Buster generation. She lived in the fast lane of life, distracted easily by the various routines of everyday living.

Jesus was not bothered by Mary's desire to sit at His feet to learn and grow in her faith. However, He gently rebuked Martha for majoring on the minor things in life. She had neglected Jesus in the name of service. Even Martha had a disposition to drift. She was disconnected from Jesus and did not even know it.

The disposition to drift that we all share can easily result in our becoming disconnected from God and not realize it. Is this possible? Remember that the Scripture says, "But Martha was distracted." The people of Israel drifted from God. Most people experience times of being disconnected from Him. This disconnection comes because we are distracted from Jesus.

The search for meaning in life is nothing new. The problems experienced by the children of Israel are the same problems of our generation. Jesus' followers were faced with the same problems we face. Everyone occasionally struggles with a lack of focus in life. As Solomon said, "There is nothing new under the sun."

Our basic problem may be that we are disconnected from God and don't even know it. However, symptoms of this problem may surface in various ways. The problem becomes apparent in schedules that are out of control. It is evident in lives that are out of focus. People are out of energy and out of time. As people strive to "keep up" in life, they find they are lagging behind.

We are just like the people of Israel in that we are prone to place the blame on others. We are similar to Martha in that we major on the minors, not taking the time to sit at the feet of Jesus. We see our problem as being the unrealistic expectations of our spouse, the fast-paced schedule of our children, the demands of our job, our lack of rest, or the lack of play we enjoy. At times we even see the problem as being the ministries and activities in which we participate in the church.

Wake up! These are not our problems. These things may be what distract us from what is really important, but they are not the problem. The problem is . . .

The Drift Away from God

As Will and Valerie entered my office, I could tell something was wrong. Tension filled the air as they uncomfortably sat down in chairs facing each other. Will was soft spoken as he began to explain the purpose of their visit. It took only a few sentences for him to share that their marriage was falling apart. As Will explained how his job had taken him away from the home, it became apparent that he had drifted away from Valerie. After a period of time, he had even begun to spend his leisure hours with his buddies rather than his wife. No longer did Will desire to spend time with Valerie. Never did he write her sweet notes or call just to say, "I love you." She was seldom on his mind.

Even Will could not believe how far he had drifted from his wife. None of his actions had been intentional. All of this had happened so slowly that he did not even realize there was a problem. Until now.

How tragic! This couple had drifted from each other so gradually they did not even know it was happening. This story illustrates a very important reminder in Scripture about drifting from God. The passage is found in Hebrews 2:1:

For this reason we must pay much closer attention to what we have heard, lest we drift away from it.

The Book of Hebrews is about the greatness of Jesus. It shares that He is greater than the prophets, greater than the angels, and greater than any sacrificial system because He is the superior sacrifice for our sins. This is why Hebrews 2:1 says, "We must pay much closer attention to what we have heard." This verse encourages us to not let these great truths about Jesus just pass through our minds. We must not be careless or make light of them. Once we begin to neglect even the smallest areas of our Christian lives, we begin to drift from God. Over a period of time, our relationship with our Father can become just as isolated as the relationship of the young couple who had sought help for their marriage.

What does it mean to drift from God? It means to slip away from Him. This drifting can be very careless, or it can be very subtle and unintentional. To drift from God means that we become disconnected from Him, although we may not even realize it. I am not saying that when we drift we lose our salvation; however, I am saying that we often become disconnected from God and His power and do not know it. This is the drift factor. The drift away from God begins when we lose our focus on Jesus. It happens when we only glance at Him, but gaze upon our circumstances. When we do this, life becomes a blur. Our goal becomes mere survival rather than spiritual power.

There are four characteristics of drifting from God. As we keep in mind the illustration of the young couple who slowly drifted away from each other, let us evaluate our spiritual lives to see if we are victims of the drift factor.

The Drift Is Careless

Many people are careless in their walk with Jesus Christ. I have never met anyone who really wanted to drift from God. But at times, perhaps, we handle our spiritual lives carelessly. Even as Will became careless in showing love for his wife in the smallest ways, we often become careless in our spiritual lives by neglecting the little things. This is when our drifting from God begins — when we start to neglect the little things.

This carelessness means that we do not value our spiritual life enough to handle it with care. Our spiritual life is fragile. We are only human and have feet of clay. We are in deep need of an ongoing relationship with Jesus. When a Christian does not handle God's things with care, however, he becomes careless in his relationship with Christ. The end result is the drift factor.

If a Christian is careless in spending personal time with God, eventually he will drift away from Him. If a believer does not give priority to the studying, preaching, and teaching of God's Word, he will drift from Him. If a Christian is not accountable to a local body of believers, then he will drift away from Him. When carelessness results in a drifting from God, the only remedy is to reconnect with Him.

The Drift Is Gradual

The drift away from God never begins with what we would categorize as one of the major sins. It begins with a gradual slide. It begins with simple negligence.

As a pastor, I have seen this on numerous occasions. Many so-called Christians minimize the role of the church. They underestimate the importance of regularly being under the preaching and teaching of the Word of God. I have observed many believers who were excited in their Christian walk gradually slide into a carnal lifestyle. When confronted, their typical response was, "I am just too busy to be in church all the time." Others are dominated by their family schedules or the unfair rule of a supervisor on their job. This neglect of the church was the initial step toward drifting away from God. One by one, people fall victim to the drift factor. They become disconnected from God and do not even know it.

The Drift Is Subtle

The drift away from God happens in the most subtle manner. Job, family affairs, personal desires, and many other things can be the subtle approach Satan uses to lure the Christian from God. I have seen strong Christians drift. Even as a pastor, I am not immune from the subtleties of Satan. We are all Satan's prey.

The drift is subtle because we do not place enough importance on our relationship with God to nurture it. When someone calls us to be accountable, we attempt to pass their remarks off as being legalistic. None of us want to be considered as legalistic. Therefore, we become victims—victims of the most subtle of Satan's schemes, the drift away from God.

The Drift Is Unintentional

We can have good intentions and still drift from God. I have never met anyone who was far from Him who wanted to be. I have never met anyone who was involved in grotesque sin who wanted to be. Anytime I have drifted from God, it was not my intention to do so. It happened only because I was careless in my walk with Christ.

Most Christians do not intend to drift; however, most of us live our spiritual lives in a state of careless, gradual, subtle, and unintentional drifting from God. We have become disconnected from Him and His power, yet we do not even know it. We need to hear the passion of the apostle Paul's plea as he warned us in 1 Timothy 4:1:

But the Spirit explicitly says that in later times some will fall away from the faith, paying attention to deceitful spirits and doctrines of demons.

It is obvious from this passage that we are close to the return of Jesus Christ. We are seeing the great falling away from the faith. This is speaking of the drift factor. However, this is happening only because of a careless walk with Jesus Christ. It is time to reconnect with God.

The Demonstrative Voice of God

An interesting study was conducted that examined the effect of the sound of a mother's heartbeat on an infant. Researchers hypothesized that during the prenatal period, a fetus becomes imprinted or "fixed" on the mother's heartbeat sound. From this hypothesis scientists predicted that after the baby was born, an auditory stimulation similar to the beat of the mother's heart would soothe the baby. To conduct the study, researchers recorded a heart that beat approximately 72 beats per minute, which is the typical heartbeat of a young mother. Using a tape recorder, they played this sound to newborns. The newborns who were exposed to the sound of the heartbeat gained more weight than did the group that had no sound played for them, even though both groups consumed the same quantity of food. Moreover, the group who heard the heartbeat cried less than the group who did not hear it. Doctors concluded that the increased crying of the latter group required a greater consumption of the energy available from the food. This explains why this group gained less weight.

Researchers extended the study to children beyond infancy and discovered the heartbeat's sound continued to have positive effects. The group that heard this sound had better socialization and relational skills and better overall development than the group without the sound. The conclusion of the study was that we, in our physical nature, are imprinted to our mothers' heartbeat. Our connection to her is a source of strength and comfort.

In a similar manner, we have been imprinted to the heartbeat of our Creator. Our connection to Him is a source of strength and comfort. We are imprinted by the person of God. Created in His image, we are in need of being connected with Him. We are in need of hearing His voice and knowing we are close to Him.

God loves us so much that He is committed to revealing to us our genuine spiritual condition. When we drift away from Him, God desires to call us back. How does He do this? He calls us back by His voice. His voice is demonstrative in that it is a distinguishing voice. It is a true voice that reveals whether or not we are victims of the drift factor. It is a voice that continually moves us back toward God.

Abraham heard the voice of God. God had spoken to him and revealed His promise of a son. When Abraham despaired that God would fulfill that promise, he drifted away from Him. It was while he was disconnected from God that Abraham began to listen to other voices. In Genesis 16:2, the Bible says:

So Sarai said to Abram, "Now behold, the Lord has prevented me from bearing children. Please go in to my maid; perhaps I shall obtain children through her." And Abram listened to the voice of Sarai.

Yet God continued to speak to Abraham. In Genesis 17:9, 15, and 16 the Bible records:

God said further to Abraham, "Now as for you, you shall keep My covenant, you and your descendants after you throughout their genera-tions". . . . Then God said to Abraham, "As for Sarai your wife, you shall not call her name Sarai, but Sarah shall be her name. And I will bless her, and indeed I will give you a son by her."

God is faithful! He continues to speak to us even when we have drifted from Him.

I have heard the testimony of certain people who claim they have heard the audible voice of God. Even though God has never spoken to me in this manner, the apostle John testified of hearing God's voice when he stated, "His voice was like the sound of many waters" (Rev. 1:15). Does God still speak audibly to His people? I would always give room for God to do what He chooses to do; however, the more important question is, "How does God speak to us today?"

The demonstrative voice of God can be heard in many ways. It can be heard through the reading of God's Word. Any Christian who wants to walk with Christ must read the Bible. It not only contains the Word of God, but the Bible is the Word of God. God has already said everything He needs to say in His Word. It is so powerful that He uses it to reveal our spiritual condition. The Bible records in Hebrews 4:12-13:

For the word of God is living and active and sharper than any two-edged sword, and piercing as far as the division of soul and spirit, of both joints and marrow, and able to judge the thoughts and intentions of the heart. And there is no creature hidden from His sight, but all things are open and laid bare to the eyes of Him with whom we have to do.

These verses assure us that when we permit God's Word to sharpen our lives daily, God will speak to us. Nothing is hidden from the demonstrative voice of God in His Word. Through the Scriptures, God calls us to admit our true spiritual condition. Then He appeals to us to enjoy full fellowship with Him by being upwardly connected with Him.

The demonstrative voice of God is frequently heard as He speaks to us through others. How many times have we listened to a person preach and wonder if he had read our mind? Sermons often pierce our hearts as we realize that God is speaking to us. Likewise, friends are sometimes used as God seeks to speak to us. Nathan, the prophet, boldly proclaimed to King David that he had sinned against God. As a result, David realized God was speaking to him to bring him to repentance. Immediately he confessed so his relationship with God could be restored.

The demonstrative voice of God is often heard through our circumstances. Since God is sovereign and faithful, He is able to use the experiences of our lives to reveal our spiritual condition and to call us into fellowship with Him.

I can be confident that if I become a victim of the drift factor, God will continually reveal this to me and call me back to Him through His Word, through other people, and through my circumstances.

The Discovery of Hope

The cars' engines raced. At the signal, the young lad pushed the accelerator all the way to the floor. The tires on his vehicle squealed as he began his new adventure. Timmy had discovered go-carts. Life was exciting those next few moments . . . until something went wrong. He saw the curve coming at him and tried to slow down. But it was too late. His car skidded into the sand that surrounded the track. Timmy managed to avoid hitting another car and came to a stop. His heart was racing as he realized what could have happened simply because he was going too fast and wasn't looking where he was going. As the small boy sat in his parked cart, feeling pretty embarrassed, he at least felt relieved that he was not hurt. The sand around the pavement slowed his car so he could regain control and return to the track. That boy decided that day in his young life that boundaries are a blessing from God.

As I have grown in my Christian walk, I, too, am grateful for the boundaries that God places around us. Because of these boundaries, there is hope when we feel that our lives are out of control. God will bring us back onto the path that connects us with Him.

Is there hope for the Christian whose life has veered from that path? Can a Christian reconnect with God once he has become disconnected from Him and may not even be aware of it? Even though all of us will face days when we are victims of the drift factor, we can be confident that God is committed to drawing us into fellowship with Him. We can be sure that God will place boundaries about our lives to slow us down as we veer off the path He has set before us. Through these boundaries, God calls us back to Him. Yes, it is possible to reconnect with God when we have disconnected from Him. The Bible contains many examples that encourage us in this regard.

In the Old Testament, King David serves as a wonderful example of God's desire to restore fellowship with His people. Even though many of us will never be victims of the sin of adultery, we can learn from David's experience, which resulted in his losing fellowship with God. Since every sin contributes to our drift from God, we can gain much insight from King David's lesson.

In Psalm 51:12 David prayed, "Restore to me the joy of Thy salvation." We know that God honored David's prayer of repentance, and once again he danced before the Lord with joy. If David can be forgiven and restored to fellowship with God, so can we. The reason for David's sin was that he had earlier become a victim of the drift factor. He had neglected his responsibilities as king by going to war. However, David discovered there was hope for him to be reconnected with God. God used the voice of Nathan, the prophet, to reveal to David the high price of his sin. Yet, in spite of his drifting from God, David reconnected with Him.

Perhaps one of the most obvious examples that there is hope for reconnection with the Father is found in the story of the prodigal son. After willfully leaving his father's house and venturing into the world, seeking a life of pleasure and independence, the son realized his plight. Could he hear his father calling him? Down deep in his soul, I know he did. It is encouraging to read that the father never gave up on his son. He never quit looking for the boy's return. In fact, when the son returned home, it was the father who was the first to greet him.

What a blessing it is to know that God never gives up on us. Hope always abounds for the child of God. There have been many times when I felt disconnected from God. I am glad that I can testify to God's loving grace that has been extended to me on every occasion. I have been very distressed at times, but God has always led me to discover there is hope in Him.

We all have this same hope. What is essential is that we examine our lives. Perhaps at this moment we are disconnected from God and do not even realize it. Even when we are faced with the tragedy of having to overcome a major sin against God, there is hope. Our hope is found in His loving grace. He forever accepts us where we are. God knows everything about us, but He loves us just the same. God is faithful. He is the God of the second chance . . . third chance . . . and yes, even when we are victims of the drift factor, we can discover the hope of fellowship with Him. It begins when we reconnect with our Creator.

This book emphasizes how we can reconnect with God in our spiritual life. Wherever we may be in our spiritual pilgrimage, we can discover that there is hope. We are never outside of God's grace. The cross of Jesus can draw us back into fellowship with God, regardless of how far we have drifted from Him. I am confident that every believer will discover hope for his life by applying seriously the principles that are contained in this book.

It Is Time to Reconnect with God

We have learned that, through the busy times of life, it is possible to live disconnected from God without even realizing it. We have learned that each of us periodically experiences this disconnected feeling. This drift from God is usually gradual, subtle, and unintentional. It happens because we are careless in our walk with Christ. We have been reminded that God speaks to us in a demonstrative way by His Spirit through the Bible, other people, and our circumstances. We have also learned that there is hope for reconnecting our lives with God.

The drift factor described in this chapter is possibly the tallest mountain any Christian will climb. It is so crucial for us to understand that God wants us to come into full fellowship with Him. Disconnectedness from God is not His will for our lives. Therefore, we must reconnect with Him.

This upward connection with God is essential to reconnect with Him. The fruitfulness of all our relationships is dependent on our relationship with God. If this relationship is going to be filled with joy and fellowship, then we must not be guilty of drifting from Him. In those times when I have sensed I was disconnected from God, I knew the answer was to get back to Him by getting involved in meaningful fellowship with Him. My prayer for all believers is found in James 5:19-20:

My brethren, if any among you strays from the truth, and one turns him back, let him know that he who turns a sinner from the error of his way will save his soul from death, and will cover a multitude of sins.

When a Christian experiences the drift factor and comes back to God, he covers a multitude of sins. This is why it is so important to reconnect with God the instant the drift factor is recognized. It is time to reconnect with Him.

However, to live effectively for Christ, we must identify those . . .

Interruptions that can lead to that disconnected feeling.

2

Interruptions and That Disconnected Feeling

I WAS SITTING ALONE IN the surgical clinic's waiting room. Listening to CNN News and reading the newspaper seemed so insignificant that day. Even though I had planned to be with my wife, Jeana, at the clinic that particular morning, I was getting somewhat restless. In my mind I began to work out the details of the afternoon's staff meeting. Every few minutes I glanced at my watch and looked toward the door that led to the surgical area.

Finally a nurse came and took me to a small cubicle to wait for the surgeon's report on my wife's condition. As I sat there those few moments, I began to sense that something seemed different. My mind had dismissed any thoughts that there could be a problem when I looked up to see Dr. John Kendrick enter the room. By the look on his face and the tone of his voice I knew something was wrong. Suddenly I felt as though I was being swallowed by the cubicle.

The words that Dr. Kendrick shared with me still echo in my mind: "Ronnie, your wife has cancer." I was used to seeing John wearing jeans and a t-shirt as he coached my oldest son's baseball team. I was used to seeing him at church greeting people with his usual warmth. It was only at this moment that it dawned on me that my friend John was a physician who had the painful task of bearing the news that would change my family forever. As soon as he shared that piercing statement, I asked, "Have you told Jeana?" He replied, "No, I wanted to talk to you first."

For almost five years Jeana's mammogram had shown a possible problem. She had gone to various doctors in the city where we had lived previously, as well as in the area where we had now lived for three and one-half years. Each physician had assured her that everything was all right. Eventually she discovered a lump in her breast. Once again the doctors assured Jeana there was no reason to be alarmed. However, two months prior to this fateful day, I had encouraged Jeana to seek the opinion of our surgeon friend who was now standing before me.

During Jeana's initial visit to Dr. Kendrick, he, too, indicated that he expected no problem. However, as a precaution John suggested that a biopsy should be performed. It was scheduled for Monday, January 15, 1990.

This morning had arrived as uneventfully as any other Monday morning. Jeana did not want me to go with her that day so I could get Joshua and Nicholas, our two boys, ready for school. However, something inside me convinced me I needed to go with Jeana, so I took her to the clinic and then went home long enough to help the boys and take them to the home of a neighbor who would take them on to school. I rushed back to the clinic to wait with Jeana through what I thought was to be a normal procedure, only a two-hour disruption to our lives.

I was wrong. The reality of Jeana's cancer took both Dr. Kendrick and me by surprise.

How could a beautiful young woman only 35 years old, filled with energy and a zest for living, have such a life-threatening disease? As the doctor shared the news of Jeana's breast cancer, my mind grasped for a plan of action that would end this nightmare. What should we do next? I told Dr. Kendrick that I wanted to get the best treatment in the world for Jeana. My immediate thought was that we should take her to M. D. Anderson Hospital in Houston, Texas. Dr. Kendrick said he would honor my request and assist us in any way possible.

The nurse then ushered me into the room where my wife was sitting. Jeana immediately noticed my facial expressions. Although I was trying to hide them until the doctor could tell her himself, after thirteen years of marriage Jeana knew there was a problem. After unsuccessfully dodging her questions, I looked at her and said, "Jeana, you have cancer." The color drained from the face of my beautiful young wife. We felt so helpless. The strong pastor and leader of a thriving megachurch became so feeble, so quickly.

The doctor entered the room and shared with us our options. He recommended that we see an oncologist, a specialist in cancer, immediately. While Dr. Kendrick was honest with us as a physician, he was comforting to us as a friend.

The nurse helped me get Jeana in the car. Before we could go home, we had to fill a prescription. We were numb with shock as we drove to our local pharmacy. We felt helpless and alone. Gradually we began to talk. Should we tell the children? What should we tell them? Does our church need to know? How can we tell them? Since I was a visible leader in our area, this was going to be a challenge for me. We knew rumors would be rampant and magnified beyond reality.

Even though we felt alone, I cannot say that we felt disconnected from God because within minutes the peace of God was with us. We knew God was up to something. We determined that we would not play games. We would be honest with everyone; we needed them. All of our family members lived in Texas, hundreds of miles away. We needed our spiritual family to support us in prayer and love during this time that uncertainty abounded and our imaginations were racing to the extreme.

After pulling into the driveway of our home, I helped Jeana into the house. This would be the first of many times that we went through this procedure over the next several months, but I was too ignorant of the future to know this would become a familiar experience. After I gave Jeana her medication, she laid down on the sofa in our den. During these moments of fear and uncertainty, we prayed together for God's strength and wisdom.

I remember saying, "This can't be. We're too young for this." In disbelief, I thought, "Hey God, I'm 34 years old with nine- and six-year-old boys. They need their mother. What will I do if you take my sweet wife?" I needed her. The boys needed her. We wanted to be normal again. Little did I know that things were not going to be normal again for many months.

Even though I felt connected with God, I now felt disconnected from the things and people around me. Other people, things, goals, and all other concerns that had previously been high on my list of priorities no longer mattered to me. All I wanted was for God to give me my wife for a lifetime.

Life is filled with continual interruptions. These disruptions can lead to a feeling of disconnection from God. The disruptions we face are many. My family faces them continually, even though Jeana's cancer was the most significant one we have ever experienced. These interruptions are varied in nature, and sometimes the minor ones lead us to feel more disconnected from God than do the major ones. A possible reason for this is that we often attempt to handle the smaller difficulties apart from God's power. The result is that we end up powerless.

In order to handle these interruptions in the proper spiritual manner, we need to be able to identify them. As we all face these, as well as other interruptions, we need to look at them from God's perspective.

Various Crises

There are various levels of crises in our lives. The bottom line is that if a problem interrupts our lives at all, we may consider it a crisis. Many people have faced a greater crisis than cancer. Others have never faced a problem that is life-threatening. Regardless of the level of one's crisis, though, it has the power to make a person feel disconnected from God.

Many people are facing a crisis in their marriage. Others are dealing with problems with a child. There is an ever-increasing number of people who are facing challenges in their job. Financial stress is existent in almost every family. Many adults are struggling with the challenge of being a single parent. Others face serious illness or the loss of physical health. Numerous Christians are dealing with a myriad of crises. As a result, many are feeling alone and sometimes far away from God. This disconnected feeling often adds to the crisis.

The story of Job challenges us to have a positive perspective of the crises we experience. We know from the first chapter of this book that God allowed Job's faith to be tested. The Bible records in Job 1:12:

Then the Lord said to Satan, "Behold, all that he has is in your power, only do not put forth your hand on him." So Satan departed from the presence of the Lord.

Every crisis we face comes to us only after God has allowed it to do so. Since God is our Father, everything we experience is first filtered through His hand.

Job lost his possessions and his family. He became very ill. His friends gave him poor advice. Job's life was filled with continual interruption. Job's faith was challenged constantly. What was Job's attitude? In Job 1:20–22 we learn:

Then Job arose and tore his robe and shaved his head, and he fell to the ground and worshiped. And he said, "Naked I came from my mother's womb, And naked I shall return there. The Lord gave and the Lord has taken away. Blessed be the name of the Lord." Through all this Job did not sin nor did he blame God.

Through all Job's trials there may have been times when he felt disconnected from God. But Job understood what was really important: worshiping God at all times.

Our society has a real tendency to blame others for our problems. Some even blame God for them. At no time did Job blame God for his circumstances. When his life was interrupted because of the losses he experienced, Job still worshipped and blessed God. From now on our first response toward any crisis should be to worship and bless the Lord. This will keep us from feeling disconnected from God.

The Fast Pace of Society

When I was a boy, almost every Saturday evening my family would drive 25 miles to visit my grandmother and other relatives. We would eat a simple dinner, sit on the porch, and maybe watch the latest episode of "Gunsmoke." Time was plentiful. No one was in a hurry. Things were calm.

What happened?

It seems that whatever happens around us or to us is accelerated because of the fast pace of society. Life is on an accelerated race toward the end. As the Bible prophesies in the Revelation of Jesus Christ, things will begin to happen in much rapid succession prior to Jesus' return. This is exactly what is happening.

People are too busy. We are too busy for one another. We are even too busy for our families. The calmness of the times in which I grew up is gone. Very few days are now given to rest and enjoyment. Why? Because of the fast pace of our society.

When we are living at such a rapid pace, it is easy to leave God out of our lives. In fact, there may be some days when we give no thought at all to God because we are so busy. This is when we feel the most disconnected from God. As we live detached from Him, our lives become powerless spiritually. Sometimes we are aware of this, but sometimes we are not. Regardless of society's rapid pace, we need to be aware of God and experience His power. His power is the only hope we have in keeping life in perspective in these hectic times.

"Survival" is an important word in our minds. Because of the rapid pace of our world, our foremost goal is often survival. Even though survival seems paramount, what we really need is to trust God for our survival. Therefore, what is the real issue we face in surviving the fast pace of our society? The real issue can be addressed by asking, "What are our priorities in life?" I will address this subject later in this book.

However, it is essential that a person take the time to experience the upward connection with God. Take time for the family. Take time for others. Other people are very important to our lives. We should never allow the fast pace of society to steal these joys from us. We are here to serve God and others, not to be victims of our hectic schedules.

Family Schedules

At times I feel like I have no time for myself. As the pastor of a megachurch which demands countless hours of my time, I am a very busy person. I am up most mornings by 5:15 and usually get home from the office no earlier than 6:00 p.m. Many of my evenings as well are obligated to ministry activities.

In addition, my family schedule is very demanding. Joshua and Nicholas love athletics. Our lives are spent going from football, to basketball, and then to baseball. Just as one sport comes to an end, the next one begins. There is no time to catch one's breath. Jeana also is busy with many activities. Following her bout with cancer, she began a ministry for cancer patients and their families. Needless to say, this takes much of her time.

Every family is now faced with the challenge of finding enough quality time together. Things are not simple anymore. Everything seems so complex.

Most fathers are wondering how to shuffle their various job responsibilities with their desire to be a good husband and father. Most mothers feel like they are running a taxi service as they haul their children to the many school and sports activities. At times, even my children would rather stay home and rest than go to a movie.

Things are moving so fast. If we are not careful, we begin to feel disconnected from God. The schedule of our families is one interruption that can lead to that disconnected feeling. Rather than living life feeling out of touch with Him, we must find a solution.

Somewhere there must be time for God. Somehow there needs to be time for one another. Someway there must be time for the family to be nourished together spiritually. How can all of this fit into a family schedule that seems to interrupt, rather than bless, our families? Later on we we will consider some suggestions that will help us achieve this upward connection with God, as well as bring order to our family's schedule.

The High Expectations of Others

Leadership is one of the greatest privileges the Lord has given me. Leadership is one of my gifts. However, there is a price to pay if a person is going to be an effective leader. As the leader of a church whose membership is in the thousands, I face many challenges. One of my greatest challenges is dealing with the expectations placed on me by my members. People have high expectations of a pastor today. If I do not keep this in perspective, I will live with the constant guilt of not being able to live up to these expectations.

Failure to live up to the expectations of others can be a major interruption in our lives. At times we may even want to give up because we know we have disappointed others by failing to meet their expectations.

When Jesus was on this earth, many people, especially the Jews, placed high expectations on Him. They presumed He had come to set up His kingly rule on earth. They judged Him constantly by their view of what He was supposed to do. Jesus tried to inform them that His kingdom was not here but in heaven. As a result, many attempted to make Jesus feel like a failure because of their high expectations of Him. However, Jesus spent time connecting with the Father in order to maintain His relationship with Him. The result was that Jesus did not allow the expectations of others to serve as His agenda. His only agenda was to do the will of His Father.

The high expectations of others can lead to that disconnected feeling, but they do not have to do so. Time with God results in an understanding of His mission for our lives. Time with the Father reminds us that we are here only to please Him. Time with God deepens our upward connection with Him. As a result of time with God, we will be able to keep the expectations of others in perspective. Therefore, these expectations do not have to interrupt our spiritual lives; rather they can contribute to our growth by pushing us into the Father's presence.

The Immoral Influences Around Us

The 1992 political elections brought to the surface the moral values of the American people. "Family values" became a major issue. Most of the American public was surprised by the strong and diverse opinions of our nation's citizens. Many people went to the polls in this election and voted for their preferential party, regardless of its platform on moral issues. Others cast their votes solely on the basis of moral convictions. Many Christians viewed the 1992 election as the election where moral values lost. In the minds of many, this symbolized the moral decline of our country.

At no time in my life have I felt like Christians were in the minority . . . until now. The apostle Paul warns us in 2 Timothy 3:1, "But realize this, that in the last days, difficult times will come." Paul goes on to mention many sins that will abound before Jesus comes again.

As a force that disrupts our connection with God, the race toward moral decline equals the rapid pace of society. There now seems to be little hope for righteousness and truth to prevail.

I frequently encounter Christians who are in a major depression over America's spiritual condition. Many had believed that righteousness was making progress, but that, suddenly, unrighteousness and immorality have taken over. As a result, discouragement runs rampant in the lives of many believers.

My friend, John Jacobs, the dynamic leader of the Power Team, says that there are three words that characterize today's youth. These words are "used, abused, and confused." I have spent hours pondering this statement. He is right!

In this day of sexual revolution, it is a challenge for our nation's youth to have a pure thought. Many are used by their friends and family members. Countless numbers of our children have been abused sexually, emotionally, and even physically. As a result, this generation is naturally confused about what is right and what is wrong. They have been taught that there are no moral absolutes. Many have seen this philosophy demonstrated in their own homes through personal abuse.

Everywhere we look we can see the moral decay of our country. In fact, these immoral influences can be an interruption that leads to our feeling disconnected from God. It appears that when righteousness takes one step forward, immorality takes three steps backward. It is easy to feel depressed over the immorality that seems to reign.

In times like these we can identify with the prophet Habbakuk when the Scripture records his feelings of disconnectedness from God. Habbakuk 1:2 says:

How long, O Lord, will I call for help, And Thou wilt not hear? I cry out to Thee, "Violence!" Yet Thou dost not save.

When the righteous suffer and the ungodly prosper, we can feel disconnected from God. Many Christians have voiced a prayer similar to Habbakuk's on many occasions. The moral decline Habbakuk observed caused an interruption in his life that made him feel detached from God. However, when he was reminded that God was on the throne and that the just shall live by faith, the interruption Habbakuk felt moved him a step toward God.

What You Should Remember About Interruptions

The various crises we face, the fast pace of society, the high expectations of others, the busy schedules of family life, and the immoral influences around us can result in our feeling disconnected from God. But these interruptions do not have to leave us with this feeling. There are things we must remember about the interruptions that come into our lives.

The apostle Paul was a person who continually faced disruptions to his life. He faced conflict after conflict. However, he never indicates that he felt disconnected from God. Instead, he appears to have allowed the interruptions he experienced to be steps that drew him into God's presence. In 1 Corinthians 10:13 we see his attitude regarding the interruptions he was experiencing:

No temptation has overtaken you but such is common to man; and God is faithful, who will not allow you to be tempted beyond what you are able, but with the temptation will provide the way of escape also, that you may be able to endure it.

What were the secrets the apostle Paul had learned that prevented his feeling disconnected from God and moved him forward into the presence of God? What lessons from Paul's life can we apply to our own lives as we are faced with daily interruptions?

Suffering Is a Part of Life

The apostle Paul knew that the temptations he faced were common; that is, they were normal. He knew that every person faces trials, suffering, or interruptions. Paul felt this was important to remember in the heat of the battle.

From my own experiences, I have learned that a person is either going into a storm, is in a storm, or is coming out of a storm. Life is filled with storms. Interruptions are constant. At times we hardly have the opportunity for a break because they come so rapidly.

Welcome to life! As long as we are in this fleshly body, we will suffer. There will be pain. We will suffer rejection and isolation.

We will even experience the feeling of being disconnected from God.

One of the secrets we must learn is that suffering is a part of life. God is not beating up on us. Our choices result in some of our suffering. Even the choices of others can result in our suffering. Our flesh is deteriorating, and this causes some of our anguish. No person is exempt. We cannot buy our way out of suffering, nor can we talk our way out of it. Depend on it. We will suffer.

God Is Faithful

Even though the apostle Paul had gone through what seems to be more than his share of suffering, he confessed, "God is faithful." This conviction of the faithfulness of God seemed to dominate Paul's life. By recognizing God's faithfulness to him, Paul permitted the interruptions in his life to make him better, rather than bitter.

One of my greatest joys is being a father. I love Joshua and Nicholas. I would lay down my life for them. I want them to be successful. I desire them to experience God's best for their lives.

However, during the times when I have to discipline my sons, I know they probably doubt whether I really want what is best for them. I am reminded of my own father who used to tell me, both before and after he disciplined me, "Ronnie, this is going to hurt me more than it is going to hurt you." As a child I thought, "Sure, Dad!" As a father, I understand.

As an earthly father I want what is best for my children. I am confident that God, my Heavenly Father, desires what is best for me; in fact, His desire is greater for me than my desire is for my children. Why? Because God is faithful. The interruptions we experience may be designed by God to prove His faithfulness to us.

God Knows Our Limits

The apostle Paul confidently shares with us that God knows our limits. He will never place more on us than we can bear. Some interruptions we encounter may challenge this truth. At times we may feel we are down as far as we can go when more trouble comes along.

I have seen this secret test many people. How can we share this truth with someone who has just lost his son in an accident? How can we share this truth with someone who has lost his daughter to cancer? During this time of feeling disconnected from God, people doubt God's faithfulness and whether He really knows their limit.

We have all experienced times when we felt, *I can't take much more of this.* Yet, frequently that is when something else happens that we are not expecting. In these times I have learned to rest in the Lord's promise that He is faithful and will never let me go through more than I can bear. He is my Father. He will give me only what is good for me.

If we are to escape feeling bitter and disconnected, we must remember that God does know our limits. His Word says that He will never place on us more than we can endure. So take a deep breath! God is faithful to you. He knows your limits. Life may be pressing, but hold on. Why?

God Will Provide a Way of Escape

God's Word promises us that He will take our interruptions and provide a way of escape. This escape will come in God's own timing. We cannot dictate to God when to deliver us. We can only trust in His faithfulness that He will never put more on us than we can bear and that, with our temptation, He will display His grace to enable us to endure it.

None of us desire to be disconnected from God. We want life's interruptions to move us toward Him, not away from Him. We want to become better, not bitter as a result of these interruptions.

The secret is to endure the interruption until God provides His promised way of escape. This escape may not come in the miracle or timing we desire. However, it will come in the way God knows is best, and it will come only in His timing. But it will come.

So, what should we do? Hang in the battle. Don't give up! Hold on to God. He is faithful! He knows your limits. He will provide a way of escape!

When my family's lives were interrupted by my wife's cancer, God's grace enabled us to become better as a result of it, rather than bitter. To God's glory, we felt disconnected from God only for a few moments. He proved Himself to be faithful and true to us.

Surely there were times when we would rather have been somewhere else. There were times when we felt we had gone through the drive-through window and received the wrong order. However, God was faithful! It was our time to walk in suffering and brokenness. This was a task I could not assign to one of my friends or staff members. My family had to walk through it personally.

I became a pastor when I was twenty years old. After a while I faced many interruptions that made me feel like a failure. I began to wonder how God could fit into the circumstances I was enduring. However, Jeana and I became friends with a wise, godly deacon who had retired in that small town where we were living. After seeing me go through some "fire" as a pastor, this wise man shared some life-changing words with me. He said, "Ronnie, as a leader, never react to others. Only respond." These words have not only provided me with an important insight on leadership; they have also provided important insight about life.

When we experience interruptions in our lives, we must not react to them. Reacting to them may result in more damage than the interruption itself. Our role is to respond to them the way the Lord would respond. How did He respond to interruptions?

Jesus always let His interruptions move Him toward His Father. They led Him to experience an upward connection with God. This is our challenge. We cannot let our interruptions push us from God; we must allow them to move us toward Him. We need His presence and His strength in order to endure until He provides a way of escape. We need to experience the joy of being upwardly connected to God, especially when we need Him the most. Our greatest desire must be to experience the upward connection with Him, even through the interruptions we experience.

But wait . . .

While we may desire to connect with God, does He desire to connect with us?

3

The God Who
Desires to
Connect with You

<small>It was late in the after-</small>noon. Our two boys were playing baseball in the big field behind our house. We heard lots of cheering and hollering and all the things that go with the fun of being with friends. I am not sure who won the ball game. It was probably one of those afternoons when keeping score was not all that important. Those young boys were merely enjoying the fun of hitting and catching the ball. Little did we realize that something happened during those hours of play that would affect my seven-year-old son, Josh, for days to come.

The next day one of Josh's eyes began to turn very red. He complained of some pain. Jeana suspicioned that he had contracted pink eye. However, after taking Josh to our doctor, we learned differently.

While Josh was playing ball the day before, a piece of the metal bat had chipped off and landed in his eye. The doctor extracted the small foreign object from Josh's eye, and within days he was fine. However, this experience led us to discover a further problem with Josh's eyes.

During the eye examination, Josh was unable to pass the eyesight test. His poor eyesight came as a complete surprise to us.

Josh's ability to see was getting progressively worse. However, he had learned to live with his loss of sight and to compensate for it.

Once Josh put on his first pair of glasses, he was amazed at the things he was able to see. Now he could see the leaves on the trees, which had been merely a blur to him. He was able to read signs along the roadside. He even could see the baseball more clearly. Josh began to see a whole new world.

As I reflect on that experience, I marvel at how well Josh had learned to make up for his inability to see. He was not even aware that there was more for him to see. His eyesight deteriorated so gradually that he did not realize he was losing his sight. However, by simply wearing eyeglasses, Josh's perspective of the world around him was dramatically changed.

When I feel the interruptions and pressures of life, my perspective of life can become distorted. If these pressures have caused me to drift from God without my realizing it, then my perspective will also change. I will not view things as I should and in time will even live with a limited perspective of God. My vision of who He is becomes blurred. This disconnection from Him is so subtle that one's perspective is changed very slowly. In the process, we adapt, just as my son adapted to his poor eyesight. We learn to live with less of God without even realizing it.

The Bible tells us much about a man who was a literary genius. He was born in 760 B.C. He had a significant position with the reigning monarchs. This man was astute politically and economically. Regardless of the issues facing his nation, he was aware of them and able to articulate about them. This man was Isaiah.

Isaiah's nation was in trouble. There appeared to be no leader who would arise to lead the nation to a commitment to righteousness. As Isaiah felt burdened about the condition of his nation, he felt the need to go to the temple to pray. Isaiah sensed that his people had become disconnected from God. He had watched them drift morally for years. He had seen their self-centeredness lead them away from fellowship with God.

One particular day as Isaiah went to the temple to pray, he had an experience that would permanently change his life. This 20-year-old man had a spiritual encounter that would set him apart as one of God's anointed prophets. This encounter was not the result of a special word from a leader in the temple. It was not even the result of his prayers to God. But on this day something extraordinary happened to this young man.

Just as my son Josh began to see things differently the day he was given eyeglasses, Isaiah began to see things differently. Isaiah saw what only a few have seen. He saw the Lord! That's right. With his own eyes, Isaiah saw the Lord. He entered the temple with a burden to pray for God's people who were drifting. He left the temple commissioned by God to share a message, even though he would face disappointment and few would even listen to him. This message would be to God's people, just as his own name meant "Yahweh saves."

What would make Isaiah a faithful prophet of God? What would cause him to be recorded as a major prophet? Would it be his incredible intellect? Would it be his political or economic astuteness? Would it be his message that the people's religion was meaningless because of their pride?

Isaiah was different. He was blessed. He saw the Lord! The Bible records in Isaiah 6:1-4:

In the year of King Uzziah's death, I saw the Lord sitting on a throne, lofty and exalted, with the train of His robe filling the temple. Seraphim stood above Him, each having six wings; with two he covered his face, and with two he covered his feet, and with two he flew. And one called out to another and said, "Holy, Holy, Holy, is the Lord of hosts, the whole earth is full of His glory." And the foundations of the thresholds trembled at the voice of him who called out, while the temple was filling with smoke.

Isaiah would never be the same. He went into the temple burdened over the disobedience of God's people. He left the temple as he saw the God who wanted to connect with His people. Isaiah saw the God who offered forgiveness to those who would repent. He saw the God who would one day express His strong commitment to fulfill His promise by sending the Messiah into this world. Isaiah's whole perspective had changed. It changed only because he saw the Lord.

Who God Is

In 1991 I had the privilege of seeing the president of the United States. I did not see him as the result of a personal invitation to the

White House, but I was attending a denominational convention where the president brought the keynote address. I had seen George Bush many times on television, first when he was vice president and then as president. But today would be different. I was going to be within 90 feet of the most powerful man in the world.

I have to admit that from that day on, every time I saw President Bush on television, I viewed him differently. I acted as though he was a personal friend. When I returned from that convention, I told everyone that I had seen the president of the United States. I shared this with my children and described every detail of what I had seen. Never will I forget that experience.

Isaiah had been in the presence of reigning monarchs before. He was familiar with their royalty and power as world leaders. But the significance of that quickly diminished the day Isaiah saw the Lord. In the midst of Isaiah's burdens for his people, God revealed Himself.

Since our innermost desire as a believer should be to experience to the fullest our upward connection to God, we need to look specifically at what Isaiah recorded when he saw God. Perhaps it will help our perspective, just as my son's eyeglasses drastically changed his ability to see. It will change the way we see things, even when we are under pressure, if we can look at the one who desires to connect with us.

God Is Exalted

Emotions were running high among the people in the convention center that summer in 1991 as the president of our country made his entrance. People were already standing. A hush fell upon the crowd as a simple introduction was given. And then thousands of people joined together in cheering and applauding this great man. The president of the United States was exalted before us on that day.

When Isaiah saw the Lord, he saw Him as exalted. The Lord was sitting on the throne. He was raised before all of heaven, in a lofty, exalted position. Isaiah had never seen so clearly the God he loved. He did not see the Lord sulking over the waywardness of His people. Isaiah saw Him exalted above all of heaven and earth.

When we feel the pressures of the world bearing down upon our shoulders, we can easily forget that God is above all the pressures of this world. He is above all the interruptions of life. God is above the problems of life. He is God. He must always be seen as exalted above everything, including ourselves. When we see Him as exalted, we can rest assured that everything is in order. He really is King!

God Is Powerful

On the day I saw our country's president, I was intrigued by those whose job was to provide security to this world leader. Television had convinced me of his easy accessibility. Not so. He was the most powerful man in the world. As never before, I realized the amazing power of our president. I sensed this power that day. I could feel it. The power of his presence was like smoke that fills a room. It was all around me.

Isaiah had also witnessed the power of his country's leaders. However, this power was minute compared to the power that he sensed from God's throne the day Isaiah saw the Lord. The Lord's robe filled the temple, signifying the Lord's majesty and royalty. When God spoke to him, Isaiah felt the large foundational stones, on which the temple doorposts stood, begin to shake. This shaking symbolized God's awesome power. Isaiah did not see God as helpless regarding the condition of His people; he saw Him as powerfully reigning over all people and all things on this earth.

When Satan attempts to deceive us by whispering, "God cannot help," we may doubt the power of God. This was not so with Isaiah. We need to learn the lesson Isaiah shares about His eyewitness encounter with God. We need to see that God is big. He is so big that nothing can overcome him. Even Satan. By the mere mention of a word from God, the world shakes. His power is potent beyond our imagination. Our problems, pressures, and interruptions are too big for us to handle. But not for God. He is the Champion of the universe. A mere glimpse of His power should bring rest to our souls!

God Is Holy

After seeing and hearing President Bush, the most powerful man in the world, on that hot summer day in 1991, I became aware of something. This man was just like me. He had two legs and two arms. He wore a suit. He even wore shoes like mine. All this merely reminded me that if our president was like me physically, he was also like me spiritually. And if he was like me, he was a mere man. Oh, he was special and powerful, but he was just a man. He had a need for God just like I did. Some may view our nation's leader as a god, but President Bush did not see himself as one, nor did I see him that way. Even the president reminded us of his humanity. He was indeed powerful; but he was human.

Isaiah must have been intrigued with the seraphim, those heavenly beings who zealously served and praised God. They announced God as holy! Three times they cried, "Holy!," indicating the complete holiness of God. When Isaiah saw the Lord as holy, he knew that God was much different than himself. There was none like Him. The Lord was above all others. When we, like Isaiah, realize the essence of God's holiness, we are aware that God does not need us, but we need God. Isaiah saw God as totally complete within Himself. This young prophet heard God referred to as the "Lord of Hosts," meaning that He is sovereign in all things. God is in charge!

Looking at God through Isaiah's words helps me understand that I have such a great need in my life for Him. I am in need of a continual connection with God that is uninterrupted by the pressures and problems of life. God is in charge of all things. My upward connection with God is the ultimate of all experiences. It is the answer to all things that tend to blur my vision of Him.

God Is Glory

On the day that I was going to see the president of our country, I got up very early in the morning. I wanted the best seat in the convention center. I wanted to be as close to him as possible. I desired to be in his presence. I hoped to see firsthand our leader as he was presented to us and as he walked into that convention center. What a thrill it would have been if I could have had a one-on-one encounter with President Bush. Nevertheless, I will never forget seeing him in person that day.

On the day Isaiah saw the Lord, he saw Him as glory. Isaiah heard with his own ears as God's glory filled the entire earth. He saw the temple filling with smoke, signifying the presence of the

Lord, the glory of God. And it filled the temple. What a moment this was for Isaiah! This upward connection was not limited by distance. Isaiah did not receive it secondhand. He was personally in the presence of this exalted, powerful, and holy God. No wonder Isaiah left the temple that day, never to be the same again!

When everywhere I look there are problems, I begin to sag under the weight of these burdens. When life seems to be filled with interruptions, I can easily lose my focus about life. However, when I am in the presence of God, things are quickly placed in their proper perspective. It is like putting on spiritual eyeglasses. I begin to see life from God's perspective rather than my own. What a relief!

As I recall that summer morning when I saw our president, I remember that I would have loved to have been closer to him. But I couldn't. Even if I had tried, I would have been prevented from doing so. After all, who was I to the president of the United States? I am only one of millions of tax-paying citizens; I'm not important to him. I was simply a single face among a mass of people.

Even though God is more exalted, powerful, holy, and full of glory than our president, He wants me to come into His presence. He does not regard me as just one among the masses. God knows my name. He even knows how much hair I have. He never places me on hold or shuns me. When I get up in the morning to pray, it's as though God says to me, "Ronnie, I've been waiting for you." Wow! God waits for me. He does not need me, but He still wants to connect with me. What a God! He is never too big to be around me, but because He is so big, He can be around me. Using Isaiah's spiritual eyeglasses convinces me that we have only seen a mere glimpse of God. But thank God for that peek!

How We Need to See God

I have heard on numerous occasions that the way we have been taught to see our earthly father is the way we will see our Heavenly Father. It is sad that many people are not as fortunate as I am. Their earthly father never loved them or comforted them with a father's touch. Their earthly father may never have met the needs they had as a child. Because many people have never had the positive role model provided by their earthly father, they struggle with faith in God as their Heavenly Father.

My dad was all that an earthly father should be. He loved me. He touched me. He was there when I needed him. He gave me gentle but firm counsel when I needed it. He disciplined me when I was wrong. He taught me responsibility and accountability. My dad met my needs.

It should, therefore, come as no surprise that faith in God comes easy for me. I have gained from my earthly father a picture of my Heavenly Father. God loves me. He wants to be with me. He desires what is best for me. He protects me. God meets my needs.

Through my walk with God over the years, I have come to know Him. I have learned more about God through the study of His various names mentioned in the Bible. We should consider some of these names in order to expand our view of who God is. Through an understanding of His names, we can gain additional insight into this God who desires to connect with us. When we understand Him, life's interruptions will be unsuccessful in blurring our vision. This understanding provides us with "spiritual eyeglasses."

Jehovah Sabaoth

As a boy I always felt that if things were to get out of control, my dad would hold them together. I viewed him as the controlling agent in our family. Now that I am a father, I realize that just as important as my being in control is my desire for my sons to think I am in control.

God is not only perceived as being in control; He is in control. When Isaiah saw the Lord, he heard the angels cry:

Holy, Holy, Holy, is the Lord of Hosts, The whole earth is full of His glory.

The term "Lord of Hosts" gives us an insight into who God is. In the Hebrew language, He is referred to as *Jehovah Sabaoth*. This is translated as "Lord of Hosts." This name of God informs us that God is all-sovereign. He is in complete control of all of life.

We should never forget that God is *Jehovah Sabaoth*. God is Lord over our greatest enemy, Satan. He has all power over everything we face. When we allow ourselves to be disconnected from God because we become consumed by our circumstances, we need to see God as the all-sovereign one. When we bow in the Father's presence, we can know He is in total control. Therefore, we can see God as yearning to connect with us.

Jehovah Jireh

When I was in the fifth grade, I saw a bicycle that I wanted more than anything. I still remember it well. It was purple and had a "banana" seat. I asked my dad if I could have the bicycle. After thinking about it for a few days, my dad bought the bike! It was the talk of all my friends. Everyone admired it. Now that I am a father, I also love to meet my children's desires. I realize the joy it must have given my dad to know he gave me what I asked.

When God told Abraham to sacrifice his son, Isaac, to Him, it must have been a wrenching experience. As Abraham laid his son upon the altar and prepared to plunge the knife into Isaac, God told him to stop. We read in Genesis 22:14, the following:

And Abraham called the name of that place The Lord Will Provide, as it is said to this day, "In the mount of the Lord it will be provided."

Abraham called that place *Jehovah Jireh*, which is Hebrew for "the Lord will provide." Abraham must have rejoiced to see God provide a ram for the sacrifice in place of Isaac.

Many people worry over whether their needs will be met. These needs may be physical, material, financial, or even spiritual. When we see God clearly, we immediately see what Abraham experienced. The Lord will provide. When we are burdened with the pressure of paying bills or whether we can honor God with the tithe, remember that He will provide for us. The name *Jehovah Jireh* provides wonderful insight into God. Whatever our need, God is able to provide. What the Lord foresees, He provides. His pre-vision is our provision. He is our Father. God is thrilled to connect with us by being our provider.

Jehovah Shammah

One of the greatest things I love about my father is that he was always there when our family needed him. Nothing distracted him from his family. My dad refused to do anything that would take him away from us. Never did he spend excessive time with a personal hobby or sport that would demand too much of his attention. Instead, he would spend hours helping my brother work on a car. He always attended my sister's band performances so he could see her march. I always knew he was in the stands when I was playing football. Dad was even there for my mother by taking her on an afternoon shopping spree in a mall. Yes, my father was always there for us.

The prophet Ezekiel had a vision of heaven. After describing what he had seen, Ezekiel concluded by saying, "The Lord is There." (Ezek. 48:35) These words come from the name of God *Jehovah Shammah*, meaning "the Lord is there." In heaven there is no temple, but the Lord Himself is there. In Psalm 46:1 we read:

God is our refuge and strength, a very present help in trouble.

These words remind us that God is here at this moment. Wherever we are, God is with us. The Lord is there. Hebrews 13:5 says:

I will never desert you, nor will I ever forsake you.

The full meaning of *Jehovah Shammah* is that He is the overflowing one, the one who is ever present with us.

Regardless of what we may face, God is with us. Wherever we go, God is there. There is no place we can go that God does not go with us. So in those moments when we feel disconnected from God, for whatever reason, we must remember that He is there. He has not moved from us. We have moved from Him. Our God desires to connect with us so much that He promised His presence wherever we would go. Therefore, even if we are at the bottom — and I have been there—God is with us. If we are at the top, God is there also. If we feel fed up with life, God is with us. We cannot face anything, good or bad, wherein God will not be there for us and with us. Therefore, we must learn to practice His forever presence in our lives.

Jehovah Shalom

I was blessed to live in a peaceful home as a boy. Oh, there were times when our family argued or disagreed, but tempers were not tolerated in our home. Anger was not allowed to be expressed in the wrong way. We had a peaceful home.

Gideon was one of the great warriors in the Old Testament. He was committed to fighting God's battles the Lord's way, rather than his own way. Gideon did not rely on reason and logic; he only relied on faith. In evidence of his faith, we read in Judges 6:24:

Then Gideon built an altar there to the Lord and named it The Lord is Peace.

The words "The Lord is Peace" come from a beautiful Old Testament name for God when he was referred to as *Jehovah Shalom*. This name means that "the Lord is our peace."

The winds of a storm may howl in our ears. Fear may grip us as we face an uncertain future. We may fret over the details of life that are not even important. The interruptions of life blur our vision. In these times we must pause and experience the peace of God. *Jehovah Shalom* is present, even in the midst of the biggest storms of life. He is present, not only to hold our hand, but to be our peace. I remember being told in college that peace is not the absence of trouble; peace is the presence of God.

Jesus

One of the exciting ministries of our church is our banner ministry. The purpose of this ministry is to make banners that lift up the many names of God. A group of ladies has volunteered hundreds of hours of their time to making these beautiful banners. Periodically these banners are brought into our worship service as we sing. As the various names for God are carried throughout our worship center, I can sense the presence of almighty God move among us. The climax often comes when the banner appears bearing simply the name Jesus. When I see this banner, I want to shout. There is something special about the name of Jesus.

Jesus is the Greek form of the Hebrew word *Joshua.* This name means "Savior." The name of Jesus encompasses all the names of God. He is the representation of the invisible God and the radiance of His glory. His name tells us what God's work is in this world. Jesus came to save people from their sins. This is the meaning of His name. There are hundreds of names for God in Scripture, but the most special of all is the name "Jesus."

What's in a name? The name represents the person. Jesus is the person who died for our sins. He is the one who gave His life as a ransom for all. Jesus is the one who was raised from the dead. He is the one who is coming again. His name is powerful. In Philippians 2:9-11, the Bible says:

Therefore also God highly exalted Him, and bestowed on Him the name which is above every name, that at the name of Jesus every knee should bow, of those who are in heaven, and on earth, and under the earth, and that every tongue should confess that Jesus Christ is Lord, to the glory of God the Father.

What else is there to say about His name? Even hell shudders at the mere mention of Jesus' name. We should use His name when we talk to God. God loves to hear it. We should sing songs that speak of Jesus' name. God loves to hear it. When we pray, we should ask all things in Jesus' name. Power is Jesus' name.

Jesus' name activates all of God's power. His name embodies all the other names of God. Jesus' name is the greatest name in all the earth.

My son Josh wore eyeglasses for a while, after we learned of his poor vision. He is now wearing contact lenses. When he wears them, he sees everything. When he removes them, everything becomes a blur to him.

In the same way, we must put on our spiritual lenses so we can see the revelation of God. We must see God for who He is. We may never experience what Isaiah saw when he saw the Lord, but we can learn from him. We can also learn to see God for who He is by understanding the various names for God. These are snapshots into His character.

God is not sitting in heaven, disinterested in us. He is not foreign to us or too busy to hear from us or to speak to us. We have put on our spiritual eyeglasses when we have a true understanding of who God is. This understanding will keep things in focus in our lives. Only when we understand who God is and how He feels about us will we not allow life's interruptions to blur our view of Him.

The God I have presented in these pages is one who is interested in us. He wants to permit us to experience Him in that upward connection. He is the God who desires to connect with us. He awaits our presence. He wants our fellowship. He loves communion with us. That is why He created us.

We must come to see God more clearly, even through the disruptions of life that often cause us to have that disconnected feeling. Then we can learn how to experience the fullness of that upward connection with Him.

He is waiting for us. It's time to take the . . .

Steps to that upward connection.

4

Steps to
That Upward
Connection

I RECEIVED JESUS CHRIST
as my Savior when I was fifteen years old and surrendered to
God's call to the ministry a year later. These events were a turning
point in my life. Throughout the remainder of my high school
years, I grew in my Christian walk. I often took the opportunity
to preach in churches across my area. However, the most significant time of my growing in Christ came when I entered college. It
was at that time that I gained the support and strength to live for
God.

From the beginning of my college years I began to grow in the
Lord at a rapid pace. God continued to change my life dramatically. Consistently I read my Bible, prayed, listened to tapes of
great sermons, and held prayer meetings with friends. My greatest
desire was to walk with God. On weekends I seized every opportunity to preach the gospel. At times I would simply go to a local
street corner and share the Word of God with a small crowd.

Near the end of my freshman year, a friend asked me to attend
a Bible conference in a nearby church. This friend's father, who
was a noted preacher, as well as other great men of God, would
be preaching. My friend felt this conference could provide the
spark that would ignite our fire for God. So we eagerly attended.

Late one evening during the conference, my friend and I were invited to have dinner with a very special man of God. This would be a time when a great preacher would challenge me. He would also allow me to ask various questions about the ministry. This would be a meaningful time!

I remember it as though it just happened. It was almost midnight as I was eating a bowl of chili. I asked this great man of God what he would tell me to do more than anything else in the ministry. He looked at me and said, "Ronnie, if you will make a daily commitment to give your first hour to God, there is no telling what God may choose to do through your life." Well, I knew I wanted to be used of God in a great way. Without even considering that I had a choice, I immediately began to spend the first hour of every day with God. Since the spring of 1975, there have been few days that I have spent this hour doing anything else.

I finished my freshman year of college, but one thing was different from how I began it. Even during the hours of studying for final exams, I was devoting the first hour of every day to be with God. I was seeking Him about His will for my life during the upcoming summer months. During this time of seeking His will, I was reading God's Word when the Lord spoke to me from Psalm 75:6-7. These verses say:

For not from the east, nor from the west, nor from the desert comes exaltation. But God is the judge; he putteth down one, and setteth up another.

These verses have been imprinted on my heart and ministry. In fact, they have become my life verses. I have come to measure all that I do, both personally and in ministry, to these two verses of Scripture. Yes, what God started in my heart as a college boy, He has cultivated toward maturity in my walk with Him.

In this chapter I will share some practical steps that have been successful in establishing the upward connection with God. Most of these steps are not new steps, but they are basic and necessary steps for any person who really desires to connect with Him. If put into practice, I believe these steps will help make one's time with God meaningful and consistent.

As I have already discussed, we live in a world that can easily distract us in our walk with Christ. The rapid pace of our society has caused many to believe the lie that we no longer have enough time to spend with God. So many believers struggle with finding time to spend with Him. Yet, it is apparent that we do make time for those things that are really important to us.

An article entitled "Too Much TV Said Problem" appeared in the March 3, 1993, issue of *The Baptist Standard* of Dallas, Texas. This article quotes Quentin Schultze, who spoke at a conference in Nashville, Tennessee, as saying:

In all the hullabaloo about television and its influence on the family, I think, we're missing the major point. The biggest influence of television is its shifting of our time usage from interpersonal relations to watching more television. Last year, the average American adult watched four hours and 40 minutes of television per day. Last year, the average American child watched three and one-half hours of television per day. Last year, the average American family had a television set on in the home seven hours per day. If we have the television on that much, what are we not doing?

One thing most Christians are not doing is spending time with God. They are disconnected from Him and lead powerless spiritual lives.

The Basic Principles

I have been an avid fan of the Dallas Cowboys for years. I have watched them play ball on television since I was a child. I've seen them win and lose. Through all their victories and defeats, I have remained one of their biggest fans. Even in 1989 when they won only one game but lost fifteen, I was still a fan. During their recent years of transition, they became disconnected from what makes a great football team. The Cowboys needed to return to the basic principles of football. During the next few seasons, this team became committed to performing these principles with excellence. The result of their returning to the basics was their winning the 1993 Super Bowl. Now they are the world's championship team.

When we forget the basic principles that keep us connected with God, we drift from Him. Once we have drifted away from God, we must go back to the basic principles that are foundational to our walk with Christ. Let us consider these simple, yet significant, principles before we look at some steps that lead to that upward connection with God.

Time

The Lord Jesus Christ should be our model in how to walk with God. In Mark 1:35 we read:

And in the early morning, while it was still dark, He arose and went out and departed to a lonely place, and was praying there.

Jesus' time to connect with the Father was early in the morning, even before sunrise. He had set aside a specific time to talk with His Father.

On most mornings I begin my time with God at 5:15 a.m. This has been my routine for many years. Am I a morning person? Absolutely not! I still have to set an alarm to wake up at this time. But this is my appointment with God, and He awaits my arrival. Since I know He desires to connect with me, I am motivated to reconnect with Him daily.

Every person must set aside a specific time to be with God. This appointment might begin with only ten minutes every day. The purpose of a time with God is simply to encounter Him, not to see how long we can be with Him. The key is to set a time and not allow anything to cause us to miss our appointment with God. I believe the morning is the best time because we are not as likely to be distracted by other events of the day. In addition, beginning our morning with God helps to bring more order to the remainder of the day. However, every person is different. What is important is that a specific time with God is planned and kept daily. If we miss an appointment with Him, we must remember that He is still awaiting our presence the next day.

Place

Jesus spent time with God in a solitary place. It was a place where He would not be interrupted by others. The setting was quiet so He could hear the Father speak to Him. The Garden of Gethsemane was one of the specific places where Jesus enjoyed the presence of His Father.

When I meet God early in the morning, it is in my office in our home. This is a quiet place where no one disturbs me. In this quiet room I enjoy the moments spent reconnecting with my Father daily.

We all need a place to which we can withdraw and spend time alone with God. This place may be at the kitchen table, at a desk, or simply sitting on the couch in a den. As we find that place to meet with God, we discover that it becomes a very special place to us.

Plan

I have found that when I do not have a plan for reading the Bible and praying, I do neither consistently. However, over the years I have developed a plan that works well for me. It changes from time to time so that the boredom of a routine will not rob me of encountering Christ.

In this chapter are some suggested plans that have been successful in helping me to daily reconnect with God. These may serve to enhance plans that we are already using. However, for those persons who do not have a method, these plans can be very helpful in maintaining that upward connection.

The most important ingredient of any plan is accountability. This is why I favor the plans that I use. Regardless of good intentions, we will not consistently reconnect with God if we have no accountability. We may choose to be accountable to a friend or a small group of persons, which is wonderful. However, it is possible for a person to develop the needed accountability within a plan even if he is not in a small group.

The basic principles of setting aside a special time, designating a solitary place, and developing a specific plan to encounter God are essential to reconnecting with Him. These foundational steps are necessary. Once these principles are in place, we are prepared to follow the practical steps that lead to that upward connection with God.

How to Read the Bible

"Do you eat breakfast each morning?" This is a question my friend and youth pastor, John Cope, recently asked his team of workers. To his surprise, he discovered that 60 percent of these workers skip breakfast regularly. When asked why they do not eat breakfast, the group's almost unanimous response was, "We do not have time."

John asked this question of his adult leadership team to teach them a spiritual principle. He shared with them that if they do not take time to be fed physically, then there is a great probability that they do not take the time to be fed spiritually. This is a good point. If the leadership in our churches fails to take the time to be nourished spiritually, then those persons who merely attend church may have the same problem. Our hunger has to become so intense that we are willing to take the time to be nourished spiritually.

God tells us in His Word the importance of the Scriptures to our lives. One of my favorite verses regarding God's Word is found in Psalm 119:11, which says:

Thy word have I treasured in my heart, that I may not sin against Thee.

The Bible should have a special place in the life of every Christian. It should be regarded as our greatest treasure. When we treasure God's Word and take it into our hearts, sin is unable to prevail in our lives.

In order for us to treasure the Bible, we must become aware of its value. We understand its value only as we read it and study it individually, in a small group, or in a worship service of a local church. When I want to connect with God, I cannot do it through other people. No one can. We must learn to value the Bible for ourselves. This is why we need to consider several ways of reading God's Word that will result in our growing in His truth.

Before we consider the various Bible reading plans that are effective, we should consider the translation that should be used. My assistant youth pastor, Shawn Smith, recently shared with me that the Bible meant nothing to him until he began to read from a translation he understood. Then the Bible came alive to him. Several translations are available. Like Shawn, every person should choose one that is easy to understand.

Since there are various ways to read the Bible, it is important that we remain flexible in our approach to reading it. Also, once we feel we are getting into a meaningless routine, we should try a different approach. Any of the following plans can be effective as we seek to know God's Word.

Reading Through the Bible in One Year

In 1990 I read through the entire Bible in one year for the first time in my life. There have been times when I started reading in the Book of Genesis, determined to make it through the Bible in a year. However, at some point I always became sidetracked and never completed the entire book until 1990. Every year since then, I have read the Bible through one time each year. How can this be done?

There are two or more Bibles available that provide dated reading for each day of the year. *The One Year Bible* has daily Old and New Testament passages, and readings from Psalms and Proverbs. By simply reading the material designated for each day, I was successful in working my way through the Bible.

Another plan that is available is *The Daily Walk Bible.* This Bible is also dated, but there is no unusual order of the passages in this plan. When a person uses this Bible, he simply reads straight through from Genesis through Revelation in one year by reading the material designated for each day. This Bible provides helps to the reader in understanding the Scripture reading, as well as a daily application.

By simply commiting ten to fifteen minutes a day, it is possible to read through the entire Bible in one year using either of these plans. Accountability is built into both plans through the dated reading.

The Thirty-Day Method

Dr. John MacArthur shared with me the thirty-day method of reading the Bible. This plan encourages a person to read through the same book for thirty consecutive days. For example, if a person wanted to read the Book of Ephesians, he would read through the entire book daily for thirty days. If a person wishes to read through a longer book, such as Matthew, he would read the first seven chapters for thirty days, the next seven chapters the next thirty days, etc., so that in three months' time the entire book of Matthew would be read. The purpose of this kind of reading is to permit the reader to catch the spirit and message of the reading to a greater degree. It also assists a person in his study of the Scripture.

The Psalms and Proverbs Plan

Psalms and Proverbs provide readings of encouragement and instruction for every believer. A helpful way to read the Scriptures is to read five Psalms and one Proverb daily. This enables a person to read through these two books once every month. This method can be a helpful addition to other Bible reading a person chooses to do.

The Bible on Cassette Tape

Some people do not enjoy reading. However, the Bible can now be listened to in its entirety through the use of cassette tapes. This means that while getting ready for the day or while traveling, a person can listen to God's Word. This can also be a supplement to a person's daily Bible reading.

If the Word of God is important, then we must find a way to read it or have it imprinted upon our hearts daily. The particular plan one may choose is not the issue. The key is to have a plan. A random pick-and-choose mentality of reading Bible passages often ends up in meaningless time. God knows when a person has a plan for reading His Word. Therefore, He is able to speak to us wherever we are in our reading of Scripture. Our daily Bible reading provides God with an avenue for speaking to us. It connects us with Him and keeps us in touch with His will for our lives.

How to Pray

My spiritual pilgrimage in the area of my prayer life has been a challenging one. Even though I have given God the first hour of my day for many years, Satan has constantly tried to distract me from this time. My prayer life has grown throughout the years. In 1989 my commitment to prayer went to a new level. One day I told God that my greatest desire was to become a man of prayer. I also shared with Him that I was tired of telling other people's stories; I wanted Him to make my own stories. Within a few months my wife was diagnosed with cancer. In the last few years God has answered my request and is making my desire to be a man of prayer a reality.

I have had to approach God just like the disciples approached Jesus as recorded in Luke 11:1, they said to Him, "Lord, teach us to pray." This was such an important request that Jesus gave it a very significant answer. He responded with what we refer to as the model prayer, or the Lord's prayer. In Matthew 6:9-13, we read:

Our Father who art in heaven, hallowed be Thy name. Thy kingdom come. Thy will be done, on earth as it is in heaven. Give us this day our daily bread. And forgive us our debts, as we also have forgiven our debtors. And do not lead us into temptation, but deliver us from evil. For Thine is the kingdom, and the power, and the glory, forever. Amen.

Is it possible that there is some meaning, not only in the prayer, but behind each area of the prayer?

The following is my plan of prayer that I practice daily. I have found it to be easy to follow and to remember. It comes directly from the Lord's prayer, the way Jesus told us to pray.

Privilege

The privilege we have is to refer to God as our "Father." This is only possible because of what Jesus did for us on the cross. This is the place where I permit the Holy Spirit to reveal sin to me. I then confess this sin to God and ask for forgiveness and cleansing from it. Then I claim 1 John 1:9, which says:

If we confess our sins, He is faithful and righteous to forgive us our sins and to cleanse us from all unrighteousness.

It is only after we have been cleansed of our sins and received forgiveness of them that we are privileged to go to the Father in prayer. Only then can we enter into a posture of conversation with our holy God whom we are allowed to call "Father."

Praise

Praise is adoring God for who He is. It is our verbal appraisal of who God is. Praise involves our loving God and blessing Him for His wonderful attributes.

The way I practice praise is through verbally expressing my love for God. This can be done through the use of His various names. In the previous chapter I mentioned some names that describe Him. These names can be used to focus on our Father's wonderful character.

Proclamation

I want my life to proclaim, "Thy kingdom come, Thy will be done." I want this message to be evident in every area of my life. Therefore, I begin this section of my prayer time receiving the filling of the Holy Spirit. I yield my mind, will, emotion, body, spirit, tongue, attitude, motives, past, present, and future to the Lord. I ask Him to control each of these areas by His Spirit. Next I proclaim the promise in the events of my life or the schedule of my day. It is then my privilege to claim the will of God for my family, my church, my ministry, my friends, and my nation. I pray that the kingdom of God will come and the will of God be done in these areas of my life and in the lives of the people for whom I am praying at this time. This proclamation is bold and can be announced verbally before the Lord with confidence that His desire is the same; that is, His will be done.

Provision

As we have already learned in the last chapter, God is the great provider. The Lord's prayer makes provision for our needs when Jesus said, "Give us this day our daily bread." Upon this authoritative word I can claim God's provision in every area of life. I can claim His provision for me personally and for my church. A person can even claim God's provision for his business. It is a great joy to know that God is able to meet all our needs.

People

The relationships we have with others are always worthy of prayer. Forgiveness is an essential ingredient of any successful relationship. The Lord's prayer makes provision for others. The emphasis on forgiveness is first upward and then outward. It all begins with God and then extends to others.

When we are having trouble forgiving someone, we must pray for that person daily, just as Jesus provided in His model prayer. It is not right to have an unforgiving spirit. We should pray for specific people whom we are having difficulty forgiving.

Power

The Lord's prayer concludes with an emphasis on God's power. His power is so mighty that He is able to deliver us from temptation. As I come to this portion of my prayer time, I claim the armor of God upon my life and the members of my family. His power is so mighty that He is the kingdom, and the power, and the glory. God is everything. He is awesome. He is power. The power of God is available for us to claim for every area of our lives. Prayer leads us to the power of God.

When God began to reveal to me the incredible truths from the Lord's prayer, I began to practice them and then to preach them to my church. After nine months of preaching about the Lord's prayer, we saw a new and fresh commitment to prayer among our people. More than that, I learned some spiritual truths that have radically changed my prayer life.

As we use this practical step, we will connect with God. Prayer is critical in the life of the believer. When we talk to God, we begin to learn that God can do more in a moment than we can do in a lifetime.

How to Use a Spiritual Journal

For years people told me that I needed to keep a spiritual journal. I never even attempted to do so until 1990. The Lord's timing was perfect because that was the year we learned my wife had cancer. From the first day of that year, I have recorded my walk with God in a journal. I would not take anything for the treasures that are contained in these written records.

Is there a scriptural admonition to keep a journal? The entire Book of Psalms serves as David's spiritual journal. We see both his good days and his bad days spiritually. Much of his spiritual life is revealed for us to read.

I want to define what I mean by "spiritual journal." This record is a daily prayer written to God. Each day I write in a small book that is dated and has a Scripture promise for that day. Since the book is dated, it provides an accountability for me to write in it daily.

How valuable is a spiritual journal? It is very valuable because it provides a person with a written documentary of his spiritual life. For example, on January 1, 1990, fifteen days prior to my wife's diagnosis of cancer, I wrote the following:

I read the entire book of 1 Peter today and will do so each day this month. My prayer for 1990 is that I will rejoice in any sufferings I face and remember the sufferings of our Lord. I commit myself and yield myself to the Almighty Lord to allow Him to exhibit His power and His life through me and be a glory through me for this entire decade. Glorify yourself through me.

This writing gives testimony to the sovereignty of God. It also reminds me of God's preparation in my life for the suffering my family would experience.

My spiritual journal is full of jewels that testify of my desire to reconnect with God daily. I am confident that the greatest spiritual blessing of my devotional life in the last few years has been the keeping of this journal. Periodically I turn to past entries and am reminded of how God has worked through my life. What a joy it is to realize that God has consistently cared for my every concern, has protected me from the fears I faced, and has provided His clear direction for my life. Without the reflecting through this journal, I might be prone to forget God's goodness to me.

Therefore, I heartily encourage every believer to use such a journal. This spiritual documentary of one's life will be a blessing. A person needs to write only a few lines, but these lines should be a prayer to God. As a person writes this prayer, he begins to experience the fullness of the upward connection with God.

Every great football team always has a huddle and always practices. These two essentials assist the team in having a success-ful game day.

We face a spiritual game every day of our lives. If we are going to win our spiritual battles, then we must find time each day to huddle with God. This is accomplished by following the basic principles in this chapter for spending consistent time alone with the Father. We must spend this time reading the Bible, praying, and keeping a spiritual journal. Our practice time comes through attending Bible studies, attending worship, listening to the tapes of various teachers and preachers, and reading books. Each of these helps equip us to walk with God.

When the pressures of life distract us from God, we must take time to huddle with Him. Through this time with our Father, we can better assess our opponent and have a more effective walk with God. The result will be a winning game day in our spiritual lives.

Many believers already understand the importance of having an upward connection with God. They may even know how to reconnect with Him by taking some of the steps described in this chapter. Since this is true, why do so few Christians win on game day? Why do so many believers fail in their desire for an upward connection with God? Is it because they do not know these steps? Is it because they are not really motivated to make these principles a part of their lives?

Many Christians have all the knowledge they need to reconnect with God. In this information age in which we live, we sometimes find ourselves almost drowning in a sea of knowledge. No, knowledge of how to connect with God is often not the problem. The problem many of us face is . . .

How to keep from stumbling over the steps to that upward connection with the God who desires to connect with us.

5

How to Keep from Stumbling over the Steps

WHEN I GRADUATED FROM high school in 1974 I was five feet eight inches tall. My weight was a lean 150 pounds. I remember my football coach placed me in the 160-pound category on some occasions, which always pleased me. Throughout college I stayed very active physically. However, in 1976 something happened. I began to gain weight.

Why does this always happen to men? Is it because the woman we marry believes she must prove to her new mother-in-law that she can cook? I married Jeana while I was still a student in college. After eating dormitory food for two and one-half years, I felt like I was feasting at a banquet every day as Jeana cooked for me. Now that I look back, I don't think I had seen real food since I left my mother's cooking. Once I was married, each meal was a treat.

During the last few months of college, my weight began to increase. However, my weight gain process really began to accelerate during my days in seminary. I was a full-time student as well as a full-time pastor of a nearby church. Exercise, therefore, had little priority during those days due to lack of time.

After pastoring the First Baptist Church of Palacios, Texas, for a couple of years, I had become a "big preacher." I was still five feet eight inches tall, but my weight had swollen to a hefty 207 pounds. While living on the Texas coast, I regularly enjoyed meals of fried shrimp and oysters. My secretary's husband owned a fish house, and all too frequently they would host a seafood feast. I pigged out each time.

One day I decided I had gone too far, so I went on my first of many diets. I was successful; within weeks my weight had dropped to 175 pounds. However, as is typically the case with rapid weight loss, it did not last. During the next few years, my weight was in for a roller coaster ride.

Finally, in 1990 I became desperate to lose weight and to permanently change my eating habits. I went on a low-fat diet and successfully reduced my weight to a comfortable 160-165 pounds. Since that time, I have maintained this weight range. What is the secret? I finally got tired of tight pants, coats that would not easily button, two chins, and the swollen look. I looked in the mirror for the last time to say, "Yuk!" I got desperate! Consequently, I disciplined my eating habits and have successfully kept off that excess weight for three years.

Millions of people in America can echo my story about dieting. Television commercials daily promote new diet plans and exercise programs. Bookstore shelves are stocked with a variety of books on dieting. Many of these books are experiencing tremendous sales. The same people often return to buy the latest program, hoping this will be the one that will give them the success they are seeking. Everyone wants to know how to lose weight.

Books that describe how to lose weight are among the thousands of titles that provide information on how to do almost anything. The how-to craze has swept America. People are dying to have someone tell them how to raise their children, how to be successful financially, how to live the Christian life, how to have a better marriage, and how to dress for success. The list is endless.

The how-to mentality has affected every segment of society, including government, business, church, relationships, and even our personal lives. People are impatient to get to the core of the subject. They simply want someone to blurt out the solution to their specific problem.

This eagerness to acquire how-to information indicates that people think there is a shortcut to everything. The "fast food" mentality has changed our expectations. People expect immediate solutions to their problems. They want everything now.

Our culture wants the delight. It wants the delight of losing weight, the delight of living successfully, the delight of being a great parent, the delight of being the ideal spouse, and even the delight of walking with God. It wants the delight of that successful product, whatever it may be that pertains to the particular interest. It wants the delight of knowing it has accomplished a specific goal.

One thing is certain regarding the how to-craze in America: whatever the subject, a person can learn how to do it. Whether it is a fix-it book for our homes or a how-to book on the Christian life, we are not short on knowledge. In fact, we are drowning in a sea of knowledge as a result of our information age.

Since there are books describing how to do almost anything, what is our problem? Surely there is a book that lists steps or actions that can provide the delight or the product a person is seeking.

In reality, we usually know the steps to take. The problem is that we tend to stumble over these steps. Whether our dilemma is a practical one at home, work, or in our Christian lives, we keep stumbling over the steps that lead to the solution.

This is especially true of most Christians I know. They know what God wants them to do. They even understand how to do much of what God desires of them. These people gear up, ready to accomplish a task, and then they "flake out." What is the problem? They sincerely want to connect with God, but they keep stumbling over the steps that will make the connection.

Knowing how to connect with God is not enough. Three attitudes that are essential if we are going to keep from stumbling over the steps that connect us with our Creator: desire, desperation and discipline.

Desire

When I became a Christian in 1971, God gave me an immediate desire to live for Him. My life was powerfully changed, even though weaknesses of the flesh prevailed many times. It has been a real challenge for me to mature in the faith, but I can honestly say that the first ten years of my Christian life were filled with a deep desire to enjoy the delight of really knowing Christ.

When I heard certain preachers share what the Lord was doing in their lives, I coveted to know Him as they did. When I heard various laypersons talk about their walk with Christ, I longed to experience the delight that could come only from the deep walk that they described. Even though I began to give the first hour of every day to God in 1975, many times followed in the years when my desire to delight in the Lord was about all I had. I often failed in connecting with God. I knew how to walk with Him, but I stumbled on many occasions.

Over the years I came to recognize that, while my desire to walk with Jesus was pure, I stumbled nevertheless; I was a lot like Peter. Peter was privileged because he had the opportunity to walk with the Savior. For three years Peter went everywhere Jesus went. Peter probably spent more time with our Lord while He was on earth than anyone. This man had a driving desire to follow Jesus. Yet, even the average Christian, when asked to recall a disciple who often failed in his walk with Christ, quickly responds by naming Peter. This is the person who is referred to as frequently "sticking his foot in his mouth." While I am not sure Peter deserves all the criticism given to him, he did stumble from time to time.

Probably the account of Peter's stumbling that is most often remembered is that which is recorded in Matthew 14:22-33. This text relates how the disciples were out in a boat late one night when the wind became very fierce. Sometime between the hours of 3:00 and 6:00 a.m., these men saw something coming toward them. They cried out, "It is a ghost." Wrong! It was Jesus walking on the water.

Peter was so intrigued by what he saw that he yelled, "If it is You, command me to come to You on the water." To Peter's surprise, Jesus replied, "Come." The disciples were dismayed, probably including Peter, as this mere man obeyed the Lord. Matthew 14:29-31 continues:

And Peter got out of the boat, and walked on the water and came toward Jesus. But seeing the wind, he became afraid, and beginning to sink, he cried out, saying, "Lord, save me!" And immediately Jesus stretched out His hand and took hold of him, and said to him, "O you of little faith, why did you doubt?"

Peter had a driving desire to meet Jesus as He walked upon the water. As he took his eyes off of Him, even for a moment, and began to focus on the waves, Peter began to sink. Yes, he did fail, but at least he got out of the boat. Even though his desire was great, he stumbled in connecting with the Master.

Would Peter learn from that experience? No doubt he learned something, at least never to try to walk on water again. But consider what else happened to this man through this experience. Peter still had the joy of being fully in the Lord's presence. This was his greatest desire.

Peter had witnessed the Lord's anointment with precious oil. He had experienced those moments of intimacy with Christ in the upper room as they had their last supper together. This man must have been angry when he heard Jesus say that one of the twelve disciples present would betray Him and another would deny Him. Peter believed he would never do either of these horrible acts. Then he left those moments of intimacy and watched Jesus as He struggled in the Garden of Gethsemane. Peter was incensed when the soldiers came to arrest his Lord.

This man walked with Jesus through the last few hours of His life. Yet, notice what happened in Matthew 26:69-75:

Now Peter was sitting outside in the courtyard, and a certain servant-girl came to him and said, "You too were with Jesus the Galilean." But he denied it before them all, saying, "I do not know what you are talking about." And when he had gone out to the gateway, another servant-girl saw him and said to those who were there, "This man was with Jesus of Nazareth." And again he denied it with an oath, "I do not know the man." And a little later the bystanders came up and said to Peter, "Surely you too are one of them; for the way you talk gives you away." Then he began to curse and swear, "I do not know the man!" And immediately a cock crowed. And Peter remembered the word which Jesus had said, "Before a cock crows, you will deny Me three times." And he went out and wept bitterly.

Peter's desire was to follow Christ; however, he continually stumbled in his relationship with Jesus. It must have grieved Peter deeply when he realized that he was the one who denied the Lord three times.

Many of us are just like Peter. For much of our Christian life we have known how to get to Jesus, to connect with God. We have known the price we might have to pay to follow Christ. Our desire is great, but we keep on stumbling.

The great thing about Peter's desire is also the great thing about our desire: at least we have the desire! There is a longing to connect with God! A desire to follow Jesus! A yearning to know the true delight of living in God's will.

We could desire a lot less. We could merely desire wealth or to be successful. We could long only for a great reputation or to have the finer things of life. But all these things will one day pass away.

Therefore, our desire is where we must begin in order to keep from stumbling over the steps to connect with God. Desire is much like hunger. Hunger is never satisfied until we eat. In the same way, our desire to connect with God is our delight. It is what we are looking for in our spiritual lives. The attitude of desire is essential to keep from stumbling over the steps to connect with God.

Desperation

After being a Christian for ten years, I moved to a new level with God. This level is what I call "desperation." God seems to permit various events to take place in our lives to get us to a point of desperation. This state is more than merely being hungry or having a desire to connect with God. A person becomes desperate when he reaches the point he knows he has no choice; he must connect with God. I reached this point of desperation. No longer could I live without experiencing God consistently.

God used various struggles in my ministry to get me to this point. He used the adjustment that comes with being a spouse and a father. God used the crisis of my wife's cancer to deepen this level of desperation. We all experience these various degrees of desperation. Through them I became determined that I had to have the power of that upward connection with God. I could not and would not live without it.

God allowed Peter to experience that same desperation. The grief that resulted from his denying Christ must have been a turning point for Peter. When Peter watched the soldiers nail Jesus to the cross, his desperation must have become more intense. When this disciple saw his Lord endure the hours of agony on the cross, his level of desperation must have surely reached the maximum level. Until Jesus died. Then Peter's desperation truly was at an optimum level. When he raced John to the grave and saw that Jesus was not there, his desperation reached a level he never could have thought possible. But once Peter saw Jesus alive again and then ascend into heaven, he was moved so greatly that he knew he must live to please this one he loved so much.

Therefore, this disciple who had days before cowered to a servant girl found himself speaking to the 120 faithful followers of Jesus. Peter had just witnessed Jesus' ascension and immediately began to tell the followers that these things had taken place. Then Peter led them in a prayer meeting.

From the beginning Peter's desire had been to please Jesus. But now his level of commitment had grown because he became more desperate for Christ. Perhaps when Peter witnessed the last events in Christ's life, he came to the point where, regardless of the cost, he was going to be everything he knew Jesus wanted him to be. Peter felt he had no choice other than to live for Jesus. But he came to this point only out of desperation.

While most Christians have the desire to connect with God, I believe only a few actually become desperate to connect with Him. It is so important for every believer to move to a deeper level with God. We must each examine where we are to determine if we are farther along in our walk with Christ than we were days, months, or even years ago.

We must consider the events that are interruptions to our connection with Him. Those events may be the pressures of life. We may consider these pressures to be problems. Perhaps we need to take the time to look at them as blessings. Maybe they are God's way of creating desperation in our lives.

God uses our struggles, interruptions, pressures, and problems to create a state of desperation. He wants us to understand that the only way we will ever live in His power is by becoming desperate—desperate enough that we reach the point in our spiritual lives that even when we consider the possible costs, we are going to go on with God.

Desire is the place where we begin to overcome the stumbling blocks that we face in our efforts to connect with God. Desperation is the rise in our commitment to the level that we refuse to let anything keep us from connecting with Him.

Is it possible to have the desire and desperation to connect with God and still stumble over the steps to connect with Him? The answer is yes. For that reason, desire and desperation must be joined with . . .

Discipline

Discipline is somewhat easy for me because of my spiritual gift of administration. Yet, over the years I have had to grow in this area. A person is disciplined when he knows what to do and makes himself do it, regardless of his attitude or feelings about the situation.

Discipline does not need to be confined to an exercise program, getting to work on time, or our performance of weekly duties around the house. Discipline is a must for a believer to live the Christian life successfully. The only way I have been able to consistently spend daily time with God is through discipline. Walking with Christ takes as much discipline as anything we do in life.

For example, the only way I can make myself get up consistently at 5:15 a.m. five days out of the week is through discipline. I know I have to spend time with God in order to connect with Him. On many mornings I have to force myself out of bed. Some mornings my flesh screams out, "You are crazy . . . you need more sleep!" On many mornings I do not even feel like praying once I do get up. However, discipline is my wake-up call! Discipline reminds me that God is awaiting my presence and desires to connect with me. Discipline denounces the flesh and focuses on the goal of connecting with God.

How could Peter have turned from being a coward to being the preacher who was anointed extraordinarily by the Holy Spirit on the day of Pentecost? God took Peter's desire and turned it into desperation. Then God matured Peter's desperation into a disciplined walk with Christ.

I am sure that when Peter began to be harrassed for preaching Christ, he considered giving up like he had done before. When he faced physical persecution, Peter probably cringed each time he was beaten. Yet, for some reason, Peter now remained faithful to Christ.

I find it interesting when I read the content of Peter's letters that are contained in the Scriptures. For example, notice what is recorded in 1 Peter 4:12-14:

Beloved, do not be surprised at the fiery ordeal among you, which comes upon you for your testing, as though some strange thing were happening to you; but to the degree that you share the sufferings of Christ, keep on rejoicing; so that also at the revelation of His glory, you may rejoice with exultation. If you are reviled for the name of Christ, you are blessed, because the Spirit of glory and of God rests upon you.

Peter was committed to helping Christians be ready to suffer for Jesus. He sought to prepare his fellow believers to be ready to die for Christ. Perhaps Peter did not want them to disappoint the Lord through cowardice actions as he had committed.

Peter called these Christians to a disciplined commitment to Christ. He had learned how to experience that disciplined walk with Jesus that would ultimately result in his enduring physical persecution, even the persecution of death by crucifixion, just like his Lord had suffered. Well, almost like his Lord. Peter was crucified upside down at his own request because he felt unworthy to die the same way Jesus had died.

Peter's commitment to Christ grew deep. His desire turned into desperation. Once his desperation was joined with discipline, Peter was an unstoppable force for God. Nothing could keep him from pleasing Jesus. He was living the disciplined Christian life.

As I have stated, most Christians have a desire to connect with God. Many have even become desperate to connect with Him. However, only a few believers have the discipline necessary for that consistent upward connection with God.

Discipline is a missing ingredient in the life of most Christians. Some call discipline legalism, which results in a mentality that excuses faithlessness to Christ. This is unacceptable. Discipline is a necessary attitude for any believer who desires to walk consistently with Jesus.

We need to stop embarrassing our Lord through our inconsistency in connecting with God. The very things that distract us from connecting with Him are multiplied when we fail in our efforts. We need to mature in our walk with Christ where we remain faithful even through the interruptions of life. We must learn to view these interruptions as God's blessings, as they force us to see our need for Him.

Is a lack of discipline keeping you from connecting with God? Is it keeping you from reaching your spiritual goals? Is a lack of discipline keeping you from spending time with God so you can know Him and experience His power? Is it the key attitude that is missing in your life?

You may have already known for sometime how to connect with Christ or perhaps you learned this in chapter 4 of this book. Regardless of when a person has learned how to have that upward connection with God, mere knowledge is not enough. Discipline to connect with Him daily, regardless of how one feels or thinks, is the essential attitude that will enable a person to experience the power of connection with God.

Just as desire, desperation, and discipline are essential attitudes to be successful in a diet, these attitudes are equally essential if a person is to experience the joy of connecting with God. We may know the steps we must take to connect with Him, but these steps must be supported and motivated by the attitudes of desire, desperation, and discipline. If these attitudes are missing, then we will continue to stumble over the steps we know to take to that upward connection.

Our desire keeps us wanting to connect with God, even when we fail. Our desperation results in our refusing to accept anything less than connection with Him. Our discipline trains us to be warriors in the battles we face daily, so that we will let nothing keep us from connecting with our Lord. All three attitudes are imperative if we wish to quit stumbling over the steps that will connect us with God.

The Upward Connection Is the Ultimate Experience

If we are able to survive the drift factor in our walk with Christ, then we also have the capacity to connect with God. We should remember that the drift factor is when we are disconnected from God and may not even realize it. This happens when we are distracted by the many interruptions that we continually face.

We become motivated to overcome these distractions and the drift factor once we understand that God desires to connect with us. It is comforting to know that even when we are disconnected from God, He still desires to connect with us. His desire to connect with us is unfailing, regardless of our lack of love or commitment to Him.

When we become aware of this God who desires to connect with us, we are willing to take the necessary steps to connect with Him. We will obey some basic principles, read the Bible, pray, and even keep a spiritual journal. Our knowledge of the steps to connect with God must be supported with the proper desire, desperation, and discipline to keep from stumbling over these steps.

The end result of this process will be an upward connection with God. This link with our Creator is the ultimate experience for the believer. As we are connected with Him, God unleashes all of His power into our lives.

Is this upward connection all there is in the Christian life? No. This connection with God is not the end; it is just the beginning. If this is so, then what is next?

Part Two

The Inward Connection

6

It May Get Worse Before It Gets Better

IT WAS IN MY FRESHMAN year of college when I began to understand what it really means to connect with God. I was growing rapidly in my Christian faith. The challenge of being in a new environment and preparing for my calling to the ministry was a source of spiritual encouragement to me. My desire to know God was thriving, and my zeal to serve Christ continued to increase. I was compelled to do what I could to win the world to Jesus Christ.

I began to sense something then that I now know for certain. When I was growing in my faith at such a rapid pace, I was becoming more conscious of my own sinfulness. At that time I could not understand why. This did not make sense. Yet I have discovered this truth. As we spend more time with the Lord, we become more aware of our own sinfulness. During those years when I eagerly wanted to connect with God, things got worse before they got better.

I would get on my knees to pray. As I prayed I found that it took a great deal of time just to work through my shortcomings. As I made an evaluation of my spiritual life, I was troubled at the sin I observed. I was an exceedingly sinful child of my Heavenly Father. In frustration I discussed my predicament with some friends whom I felt had developed a strong walk with Christ. To my dismay they told me not to worry about my sin because these sins had already been forgiven. This really confused me because I knew confession and forgiveness are important in every believer's life.

Through personal Bible study and listening to audio tapes of several preachers, I learned that the closer I would get to Jesus, the more aware I would be of my sinfulness. Therefore, I began to realize that in my efforts to connect with God, things often get worse before they get better. My desire to connect with Jesus was good. However, I discovered that part of that good process would be the consciousness of all the sin in my life. But as the result of this awareness of sin, I was able to repent of it and confess it to my Heavenly Father. Ultimately this was wonderful because it allowed me to grow in my spiritual walk in Christ.

As I began to minister as a pastor, I thought every believer was as excited as I was and wanted to be used by God to touch the world for Jesus Christ. I learned quickly that many Christians are not interested in touching anyone. Instead, they often become instruments that Satan uses to attack the gospel's progression. This reminded me of what I had learned during my freshman year in college. That is, when we become closer to Jesus, even in the church, things seem to get worse before they get better. As we experience God's power, we find that we also endure Satan's attacks. Through the years this realization has been a tremendous challenge for me. However, I have come to understand that living for Christ is a struggle. This struggle affects individual believers as well as the church corporately.

A person would easily think that when we achieve upward connection with God, our struggles are over. But this is not the case. When we connect with God, we then become aware of who we are. Sometimes this revelation is not a pleasant thing to see. In fact, when we see who we really are, we realize that things may get worse before they get better.

The prophet Isaiah experienced this truth. In Isaiah chapter 3, we find that Isaiah became aware of the God who desired to connect with Him. He was awestruck by this revelation of God. Surely after Isaiah saw the Lord, he never faced another struggle.

Wrong! Seeing the Lord in person was only the beginning of his problems. Things got much worse for Isaiah before they got better.

When Isaiah experienced the upward connection with God, he then had to experience the inward connection with himself. He had to deal with the reality of who he was, both the good and the bad. While it is often painful for a person to have to deal with who he is, it is a necessary part of the process if he wants to connect with God.

In this section of this book, we will discuss the inward connection. Only when we connect upwardly with God can we connect inwardly with who we really are. As we experience this inward connection, we will go through the same experiences of Isaiah. We will also become aware of . . .

The Reality of Our Sinfulness

Memories of my teenage years include the night my parents shook me from a sound sleep and ordered me to get up immediately and go into the hallway with them. I rubbed my eyes, struggled to my senses, and drug out of bed. I had no idea why my sleep was being disrupted, but I obeyed my parents' order. As soon as I stepped into the hallway, the window beside my bed shattered. Glass covered the place where I had been lying.

I will never forget the darkness and fear of those next few moments as I knelt in the hallway with my parents. We could not see anything. We could only hear what was happening. We heard the powerful wind. We listened as windows broke in our house. We sat silently as fragments of our roof were peeled off. The rains pounded the shingles. We were experiencing a Texas tornado.

This was a new experience for us. We had weathered hurricanes, but we always knew when to expect them and how powerful their intensity would be. Hurricanes always came with a warning. Not so with this tornado. It came from nowhere.

It seemed like the tornado lasted for hours, but it actually passed over as quickly as it had arrived. The minute it was quiet outside, we scrambled to turn on the lights. There were none. The connection to the lights had been broken and we could hardly see anything. In the calmness that followed the storm, my dad and I walked around the house. In the middle of that black night, we solemnly did the best we could to survey the damage that had been done.

I remember how relieved I was when the connection with the lights was restored a while before dawn. We were able to assess the internal damage to our house. I learned then that the better the connection, the more problems we could discover. And there were many problems to be uncovered. It was not until the sun appeared that we were able to evaluate what had been done to the outside of our dwelling.

This is the way it is when we are successful in our upward connection with God. When we see the Lord of light in His glorious power and who He is, then we become aware of the problems in our own lives. This realization of our sinful condition is often painful. But the inward connection begins with our becoming aware of who we are spiritually in light of who God is.

Isaiah had this same experience when he saw the Lord. Notice what happened to him once he saw the Lord God in His power and might:

Then I said, "Woe is me, for I am ruined! Because I am a man of unclean lips, and I live among a people of unclean lips; for my eyes have seen the King, the Lord of hosts." Then one of the seraphim flew to me, with a burning coal in his hand which he had taken from the altar with tongs. And he touched my mouth with it and said, "Behold, this has touched your lips; and your iniquity is taken away, and your sin is forgiven." (Isa. 6:5-7)

As we can see, Isaiah's seeing the Lord was not just a glorious experience. He then had to deal with the reality of his sinfulness. When Isaiah looked inward, his situation got worse before it got better. This will be true for us as well. When we look inward, what will we see about ourselves?

We Are Sinners

When Isaiah saw the Lord, he became aware of his unworthy state as a sinner. He wanted to join with the seraphim in their song about the holiness of God, but he could not. He was unworthy because of his sinfulness. In humility Isaiah admitted his sinfulness to God. He knew he was unclean, and his impurity became paramount in his mind. Isaiah's attitude, actions, and words reflected his sinful nature. His unclean words demonstrated what was in his heart. This prophet did not see himself as a privileged character because he saw the Lord; he identified himself as being sinful just as his people were sinful. Without a doubt, Isaiah recognized that he was a sinner.

When we are filled with pride, it is evident that we have not been with God. When arrogance is reflected in our spirit, it shares with everyone that we are not really connected with God or ourselves. As a superior attitude is demonstrated to others and we claim that we are without sin, it is obvious we have not been with God. The upward connection with God will lead to a definite connection with our inner person. We will view ourselves as sinners, not as successful.

We are sinners. This is something we must never forget. We are sinners by our natures. We are sinners by our choices. We are all sinners who continually fall short of the glory of God. Even though we may have been saved from the penalty of our sins, we are still sinners. When we connect upwardly with Jesus, we will connect inwardly with ourselves by seeing ourselves as sinners.

We Are Judged

Isaiah had just pronounced judgment on the nation. He was God's prophet to his people, and he gave them no slack whatsoever. However, when Isaiah saw the Lord, it was not the nation that he saw being judged; he saw the judgment of himself. This man pronounced judgment upon himself when he said, "Woe is me." He realized this judgment was upon himself because of his sinfulness and uncleanness before God.

We are still judged for our sinfulness. We will be judged eternally if we do not accept the forgiveness of Jesus Christ that He offers for our sin. A penalty must be paid for our sins, and someone has to pay this penalty. This is why Jesus came. He came to pay for our sin. If we refuse to let Jesus be the sacrifice for our sins, then we will be judged eternally for our sin in a place called hell. If we receive God's forgiveness for our sin, then Jesus' death on the cross serves as God's judgment upon our sin.

If you would like to receive God's forgiveness for your sin, I encourage you to do so right now. You can receive His forgiveness by praying the following prayer. If you will mean this prayer in your heart and speak it aloud with your lips, Jesus will become your forgiveness, your substitute who was judged for your sin. I encourage you to stop and pray the following prayer of forgiveness right now. If you do, you will live forever in a place called heaven.

Dear Lord Jesus, I know I am a sinner. I know that I do wrong every day of my life. I turn from my sin right now. I open up my life to you now and receive God's forgiveness for my sin. By faith I receive Jesus Christ into my life. Thank you for saving me from my sins. Thank you for being the sacrifice for my sins. Thank you for coming into my life. I will live for you forever. Amen.

If you prayed this prayer to God and meant it in your heart, then Jesus Christ just came into your life. Welcome to God's family of faith. You will no longer be judged for your sin because you have accepted God's judgment upon your sin by what Jesus did on the cross for you.

Once we understand what it really means to receive Jesus into our lives, it is important that we still see ourselves as sinners and as judged. The only difference is that Jesus has paid the price for our sin by receiving the judgment of our sin upon His life.

We have seen in Isaiah's life, as well as in our own lives, that when he connected upwardly with God, things got worse before they got better. Why is this so? Because he became aware of his sin. We, too, have to face the reality of our sinfulness.

Take a moment and meditate on the reality of your sinfulness. As sinners, we are depraved. We are not getting better; we are getting worse. The only good and holy thing about us is what Jesus is able to do within our lives. When we truly worship God in His holiness, we become aware of our sinfulness. As we continue to look at God in His holiness, what else do we become aware of?

The Process of Brokenness

Throughout my spiritual life, God has been working in me His process of brokenness. He has used the many disappointments of my life as a part of this process. Yet, I can honestly say that it was not until 1989 that God began to deal seriously with me in the area of spiritual brokenness.

Prior to 1989 God had begun to crack the hard shell of my flesh. He had used a myriad of events to continue the process of brokenness within me. But when my wife was diagnosed with cancer in 1990, God succeeded in shattering the remaining layers of flesh that separated my will from His. As I drew close to Jesus in prayer during this time, He revealed to me my exceedingly sinful state. I began to see that God was going to use this experience to break me spiritually.

For several years of my ministry I had the privilege of knowing Manley Beasley, a very special man of God. While I did not know him as a close personal friend, I did know him. Manley is now in heaven with Jesus, but his life impacted me in a great way. Manley Beasley was known for his great faith, especially during his battle with disease that threatened his adult life for years. One morning he called to ask how Jeana was doing. As he talked with us about her cancer, Manley also shared with me about brokenness. He prayed the following prayer for me:

Ronnie, my prayer for you and your wife is for you to get out of this all God wants you to get.

I will never forget his words. God answered Manley's prayer and used it in my life.

I learned through Jeana's illness that God has a plan for each of us. He has a process that enables us to accomplish that plan. God uses brokenness to bring us to an end of ourselves. The process He allows to accomplish this brokenness varies from person to person. For me, Jeana's cancer and the thought of losing her was what shattered my flesh. I wanted God. Other things became insignificant to me. More than anything I wanted to experience the fullness that comes only through that upward connection with Him, even though it would lead me to a process of brokenness. I wanted to learn from this experience of brokenness all that God wanted me to learn.

I have come to realize that brokenness is not a one-time event; it is a continual process. I never experience it completely so that I never have to endure it again. Instead, every time I get before God, I am reminded of my sinfulness. This brings about brokenness in me again. Therefore, as long as I am experiencing the upward connection with God, I also become inwardly connected so that I must continually deal with who I am.

This is the process God used in Isaiah's life. When Isaiah saw God in His holiness, he was broken. Isaiah was proclaiming his deserved judgment and the reality of his spiritual condition. He knew that his life would experience a continual process of brokenness. Isaiah realized that God wanted to use him in a great way, but he also knew this would be impossible until God deepened His work in Isaiah's life through spiritual brokenness.

We see the brokenness this great prophet suffered through his helpless condition. We can also see this brokenness as he was emptied of pride and arrogance. Isaiah ceased preaching to the nation, pronouncing God's judgment on them, and began to pronounce this judgment upon himself. A broken man is a humble man. A broken man is a helpless man. A broken man is a willing man. Isaiah's life illustrates all these things.

God wants to use every experience of our lives to bring about spiritual brokenness. We must learn to see each of these experiences as God's tool for accomplishing this purpose. Our challenge is to learn the lesson God wants to teach us.

Just as Isaiah saw a God who was all-sovereign, we need to see Him this way as well. This means that God is in absolute control of everything. He is able to use every incident that happens to us and around us to perform the continual process of brokenness.

Each of us will better cope with the interruptions and pressures we face if we view them as coming from God. He permits all adversity to come as a process of brokenness. He is never taken by surprise by any of these things; instead, He wants to use them to break us. Therefore, if we face illness, disease, pain, disappointment, discouragement, injustice, trouble, trial, or any kind of tribulation, we need to see that it comes from His hand. We must ask ourselves, *What is God trying to teach me through this?* This kind of response to brokenness is godly and is the way to really get in touch with who we are.

Why does God want to break us? I believe there is one major reason God is continually seeking to break us: He wants us to come to an end of ourselves. Coming to an end of ourselves will make us realize our need for God and His power more than ever before. At this point, God's power can easily flow through us. This is the power of upward connection that leads to inward connection.

A good result comes when we connect within ourselves, so even though I have emphasized the fact that things may get worse before they get better, with patience they will get better. How is this so?

The Blessing of Our Forgiveness

My youngest son, Nicholas, is a very tender-hearted child. His heart is very sensitive to God. I pray that he will always remain this way.

When Nicholas does something wrong and is made aware of it, he immediately becomes emotionally broken. Until he confesses his wrong to God and asks forgiveness, Nicholas' countenance reflects his spiritual brokenness.

Once Nicholas has prayed and received forgiveness of his sin, his countenance immediately reveals the change in his heart. This is also the way it is when he knows he has done something wrong to someone. When Nicholas asks them to forgive him, his face quickly reflects their forgiveness. Why does this happen? Because of his tender heart.

When we have a tender heart before the Lord, we will be broken when we realize our sinfulness. The blessing of forgiveness will also be reflected in our lives. In fact, the greater the realization of the sin in our lives, the more blessed is the receiving of forgiveness.

This is what Isaiah's life was like when he received God's forgiveness for his utter sinfulness. When he confessed his sin to God, the Bible says that a seraph, one of the ministers of God, took a burning coal from the altar with a tong and touched Isaiah's mouth. In that moment Isaiah experienced something remarkable.

The Removal of Guilt

As Isaiah was touched with the coal, he became cleansed of the guilt of his sin. He knew he was free from the inner tugging of his soul that was filled with guilt before God. He experienced the complete removal of uncleanness. This feeling Isaiah experienced was the blessing of God's forgiveness.

When we receive God's forgiveness, we also experience the joy of having our guilt removed. No longer do we bear the judgment of our sin, because now Christ does. The inner war that rages because of guilt is turned to an inner peace that comes only from the blessing of forgiveness. When guilt is removed, any debt we would need to pay for our sin is also removed. What a joy it is to know that we have been freed from our guilt once we receive the blessing of forgiveness.

The Removal of Sin

Isaiah was privileged to have his iniquity removed and his sins forgiven. Once he confessed his sinfulness to God, it was removed from him. In effect, God cancelled out his sin. He erased it from Isaiah's life, never to remember it again. As the Bible tells us, God took this sin and separated it from Isaiah as far as the east is from the west. As God removed Isaiah's sin, Isaiah experienced the blessing of forgiveness. We will see in the next section of this book that Isaiah was then ready to face a new challenge.

When we receive the blessing of God's forgiveness, our sin is also removed. Our slates are wiped clean. Our sin is cancelled, and we are able to begin again with God.

God's forgiveness is sufficient for all our sin. It does not matter what is in our past; God can forgive it. Even if others rate our sin as severe; God can forgive it. We need to be freed from the past guilt of our sin because God can forgive it.

God's forgiveness is powerful, regardless of how strong a hold the sin may have on us. Satan can get his claws into us, but God has enough power to free us from Satan's hold. Even when sin has a powerful grip on our lives, God wants us to realize all we need to do is simply release it to Him. Why? Because God's power is greater than all sin. This is the blessing of God's forgiveness.

To the newly formed church at Pentecost, no person was a greater threat than a man named Saul. He constantly breathed threats to those who believed in Jesus. Saul was present at the stoning of Stephen and watched him die. From there, Saul continued his selfish agenda, which was to stamp out Christianity from the first-century world. I can not think of anyone who better pictures a life gripped by sin than this man named Saul, a man who delighted in killing Christians.

However, one day on the road to Damascus, a bright light shined forth from heaven. It was God! In this moment Saul experienced a personal revelation of Jesus Himself. Through this incident, Saul lost his physical eyesight, but he could now see spiritually. He saw his need to turn from his sins and follow Jesus. Saul was miraculously changed by God's power. He received the life-changing power of forgiveness for all his sins, even the sin of killing Christ's followers. We know that shortly thereafter Saul's name was changed to Paul.

No longer was there any pride in his life. As Paul upwardly connected with God and saw the Lord, he received forgiveness of his sins. Following his miraculous conversion to Christianity, Paul began to tell everyone about Jesus. He became the leader of the missionary movement and sought to take the gospel to the entire world. Considering the rapid success he experienced, Paul could have easily become puffed up with pride. But he didn't. Paul would never forget the revelation of Jesus that God had shown him.

This is why Paul was a broken man. After Christ came into his life, Paul said, "I feel like I am less than all the apostles." As he grew in the Lord, he later stated, "I feel like I am less than the least of all the apostles." As Paul continued to mature in Christ, he stated before his death, "I am the chiefest of sinners."

Notice through these statements the process of spiritual brokenness in Paul's life. What a great example he is for us to follow. He saw himself as one who was less than anyone else; yet he was spiritually anointed and powerful. Paul proclaimed that through his weakness Christ would be made strong. What a testimony!

Paul also knew much about the blessing of forgiveness. He would never forget how Christ removed his sin and his guilt. He understood better than any other person about the powerful grace of God that provided forgiveness of sin. The blessing of forgiveness is greatest to those who have much to be forgiven. The greater the sin, the greater is the blessing of forgiveness.

Paul's life was never easy. His life was much like Isaiah's. His life was just like ours. At times things seem to get worse before they get better. When we are successful in connecting upwardly with God, we become aware of our sinful condition spiritually. This is always a painful process. It involves our seeing our sinfulness and becoming broken. But it also involves the blessing of forgiveness. This is when a person experiences the inward connection.

Since sin seems to haunt us continually, we tend to disconnect from God more than we want. When this happens, we can easily lose something very special to us. Therefore, what we will learn in the next chapter is very important to our survival in the Christian life. What is it?

7

How to Renew Your Passion for God

IT WAS IN THE SPRING OF 1975 near the end of my first year of college. As I came out of the Student Union Building, I saw a very pretty girl. She was just over five feet tall and had brunette hair. I could tell she was an unusually happy person. Immediately I was drawn to this girl and wanted to get to know her.

I learned that her name was Jeana, and she was a music major. She had just accumulated enough hours to be classified as a senior. I will never forget meeting Jeana that night. Within days I was able to spend some time with her and to get to know her better. However, I soon learned that she was already involved in a relationship with a young man. This fact, plus the fact that Jeana was a senior, meant that she would probably have no interest in me.

Shortly after I met Jeana, school dismissed for the summer. She was going to serve as a summer missionary. As we left school, I did everything I could to let her know of my interest in her. I knew beyond a doubt that Jeana had all the qualities I had ever wanted in a girl. She was the one I had been searching for; she just did not yet know it.

The summer passed slowly, but the time finally came to return to school. I was eager to see Jeana. Two good things had happened since I had first met this beautiful girl. The first was that Jeana was no longer dating the young man she had been going with in the spring. Secondly, I was now a sophomore! Surely Jeana would be impressed by that fact. She began to go out with me shortly after the fall semester began. Within days I fell in love with her. There was just one problem. She was a little slower coming to an understanding that she loved me. Jeana was a preacher's kid, and she had always said, "I'll never marry a preacher."

When the semester ended and I went home for Christmas, I made arrangements for Jeana to come to my home and meet my parents. She arrived just before New Year's. I will never forget the excitement that I felt. I knew I had to tell her my feelings, and I was just hoping she felt the same way. On New Year's Eve night I shared with this girl of my dreams, "Jeana, I love you." I couldn't believe it when she said to me, "Ronnie, I love you." We were married exactly twelve months later on December 31, 1976.

I remember that when I fell in love with Jeana during the fall of 1975, I wanted to be with her all the time. Nothing was more important to me. It was wonderful to finally be married to her because I no longer had to escort her to her dorm each night and then leave. Now she was my wife. Jeana and I enjoyed a honeymoon love as much as any couple could. We were excited about our marriage and looked forward to every aspect of our lives together.

It was only a matter of months, though, before I began to do what many husbands do. I began to take Jeana for granted. This is not a wise thing for any man to do, especially when his wife is the one who is working full time so he can complete his college education. I never really neglected my wife in a major way. It was just in those little things that I began to take her for granted.

I remember that occasionally Jeana would say, "I sure wish you would treat me like you did when we were engaged and first married." Those words hurt, but down deep I knew she was right. It was never my intention, but after a while I lost my passion for my wife. I would often ask her to forgive me and would assure her that I would try to do better. Each time I felt the need to renew my passion for her. I deeply desired to rekindle the passion and love we had experienced on our honeymoon. I wanted my love for her to remain enthusiastic, fervent, and exciting.

Through the years there have been many times when I had to renew my love for Jeana. I am sure she has had to do the same for me. In any relationship it is easy for a person to take for granted the one he loves deeply. That person then ceases to do the little things that make the relationship special. It is as though we drift apart, often without realizing it. When we become aware of this, we do everything we can to restore the honeymoon love.

The same thing can happen in our relationship with God. If we become a victim of the drift factor—being disconnected from God without even realizing it—then we can lose our passion for God. This happens when we stop doing the little things that are important to Christ. The result is that we lose the kind of love for Him that we had when we first met Him in salvation.

This is why it is important for us to daily evaluate our spiritual lives. We must continually ask ourselves, *Have I drifted from God and not even realized it? Have I lost my enthusiastic love for Jesus? Am I together inwardly so that I am able to enjoy being upwardly connected with God? If I am going to maintain this upward connection with Him, am I in touch with that inward connection with myself so that I understand where I am spiritually?*

In his book *Loving God*, Charles Colson describes how our culture has embraced the worship of fame, success, and materialism. He says that we have embraced these things because we do not know how to love God. Colson then defines what it means to love God. He states:

Loving God is a passionate desire to obey and please God, a willingly entered into discipline.

He goes on to say that the key to loving God is knowing and obeying the Word of God. Without a doubt, Colson has pinpointed what is possibly the major problem in the lives of Christians today: the need to love God!

When I met Jesus as my Savior and Lord, I had a passion for Him. I had an enthusiastic love for Christ. My number one goal was to obey and please Him, regardless of the cost. However, as time passed, I found it difficult to maintain this kind of love because of the many interruptions I experienced. Finally I realized that the only way I could keep my passion for God was by becoming disciplined in every area of my life. Even now I find that every time I fail to be disciplined, I lose my passion for God.

In the second chapter of Revelation, we read about a group of believers who had this same problem. They struggled because they had lost their passion for Jesus. We read about their struggle in Revelation 2:1-7, which says:

To the angel of the church in Ephesus write: The One who holds the seven stars in His right hand, the One who walks among the seven golden lampstands, says this: "I know your deeds and your toil and persever- ance, and that you cannot endure evil men, and you put to the test those who call themselves apostles, and they are not, and you found them to be false; and you have perseverance and have endured for My name's sake, and have not grown weary. But I have this against you, that you have left your first love. Remember therefore from where you have fallen, and repent and do the deeds you did at first; or else I am coming to you, and will remove your lampstand out of its place—unless you repent. Yet this you do have, that you hate the deeds of the Nicolaitans, which I also hate. He who has an ear, let him hear what the Spirit says to the churches. To him who overcomes, I will grant to eat of the tree of life, which is in the Paradise of God.

From this passage we learn how we can renew our passion for God. We need to begin with . . .

A Provocative Spiritual Examination

One of the most difficult things we do is make ourselves go to the doctor when we do not believe we are sick. Forcing ourselves to get an annual physical examination is usually a real challenge. As the doctor evaluates our chart, he asks some interesting ques- tions. In fact, after a few of these questions, we may begin to feel sick. As the physician puts us through the examination process, he often concludes with some provocative questions about our condition. At this point a person may begin to wonder if the doctor knows something that he is not telling. Even though this is not one of life's most enjoyable experiences, it is necessary for us to maintain good health.

Just as a physical examination is important for one's health, a spiritual checkup can result in a more meaningful walk with Christ. There are interesting statements contained in the second chapter of Revelation that we should consider. These statements provide us with a thorough spiritual examination. The process may be as distressing as the experience endured in a doctor's office. However, it is vital if we are to maintain our passion for God. Every believer must continually go through this examination by considering the following provocative statements.

We can have a great worldly and spiritual heritage and lose our passion for God. In the first-century world, Ephesus was a large metropolitan city in the Roman province of Asia. It was the most prominent city of that day. Ephesus was the home of Artemis, the Greek moon goddess, who watched over the nature of both humans and animals. The Temple of Artemis was built in Ephesus and soon became known as one of the seven wonders of the world.

During one of the apostle Paul's preaching tours, he went to Ephesus. There he discovered some followers of Jesus. Paul enjoyed his visit there so much that he stayed for three years. Many people believe that Timothy eventually became pastor of the church at Ephesus and was succeeded by the apostle John. John was the vehicle which God used to get His message on paper.

We know that the people of Ephesus had been blessed by receiving the promise of God's Spirit They were a church that had made an impact on their culture. Paul denounced the Temple of Artemis. A silversmith named Demetrius became angry because Christianity was hurting his business of making the idols of Artemis. Even though this church had at one time been effective in changing its world, Jesus later told them that they did not love Him like they used to love Him.

Just as the Christians in Ephesus had both a great worldly and spiritual heritage but lost their passion for God, this can be true of us. We live in what most people believe to be the greatest country in the world. America is more powerful than any other nation. We have more opportunities for spiritual growth than any people in the world. Many of us were raised in strong Christian homes and, in turn, are committed to teaching our families spiritual truth. However, even though we have a great worldly and spiritual heritage, many of us have lost our passion for God.

As we continue our spiritual examination, we also discover from this passage in Revelation chapter 2 a truth that has the potential of being a reality in each of our lives . . .

We can be outwardly committed to the things of God and lose our passion for God. The believers in the church at Ephesus were working for Jesus Christ. They were not lazy; they were dedicated to doing the work of God. These people were living in difficult times; yet they were outwardly committed to the things of God. Somehow, even in their commitment, these believers lost their passion for God. This seems impossible to do, but it is not.

This provocative statement is a strong commentary on many Christians today. We can attend church regularly and yet lose our passion for God. We can be a leader in the Christian community and still lose our passion for God. We can even stand for righteousness among all the immorality around us but lose our passion for God.

Even as a pastor I have experienced times when I lost my passion for God. It can still happen to me, and it can happen to you.

As we continue with our spiritual examination, consider the next provocative statement.

We can be fundamentally and doctrinally correct and lose our passion for God. The church in Ephesus did not tolerate any heresy. When they discerned that a person was a false prophet, this church dealt immediately with that person and withdrew fellowship from him. The Nicolaitans were good examples of this. These people had immoral teachings and practiced idolatry. They tried to conquer the believers at Ephesus through their teaching. Yet Jesus commends the church at Ephesus for hating the deeds of the Nicolaitans. This church was fundamentally and doctrinally correct, but somehow these believers lost their passionate love for Jesus. The very one they stood for was the one from whom they had drifted spiritually.

Today the pagan culture of America constantly questions the truthfulness of God's Word. Even some religious, so-called Christian groups challenge the truthfulness of all God's Word. The church of Jesus Christ must boldly defend the fundamentals of the faith. We must never compromise the great doctrines of the Bible.

Yet, in our battle for the faith, we must never be disconnected from the one whose faith we are defending.

If we drift from Christ, we will lose our love for Him. What a disappointment we must be to the Savior when we are on the front lines of the battle, standing for the truthfulness of God's Word, and we don't stand in love. We must love Jesus. We must love others, including the enemies of the faith.

At times I have forgotten this simple truth. Perhaps, at times, you have forgotten it also. We must remember that if we do not have love, we are like a "clanging cymbal." We may make a lot of noise but have limited influence. This can result in . . .

A Tragic Spiritual Reality

When we fail to have a regular physical examination, we may end up losing our health. Something could be wrong with us without our realizing it. I have often heard stories of people who outwardly appeared to be in good health. Yet when these same people went to the doctor, they were told, "I hope it is not too late to help you." These people had ignored or tolerated certain symptoms that should have been a warning to them. This type of negligence has often resulted in physical tragedy.

The church at Ephesus appeared to be in great shape spiritually. The people were doing what everyone around them expected them to do. Yet Jesus diagnosed them with one major spiritual problem. They had abandoned their first love. Jesus wanted them to love Him like they did the first day they found Him. He wanted their enthusiastic, fervent, passionate, personal, and endearing love. The tragic spiritual reality was that their love for Jesus had grown cold. Years before they had fought the good fight; they had kept the faith. But now they had lost their honeymoon love for Jesus, the kind of love they had when they first met Him.

Some time ago God revealed to me through this Scripture that I had abandoned my love for Jesus; I had stopped loving Him as I did when I first met Him. I was still standing for righteousness and against sin. However, I was being distracted spiritually, which resulted in my drifting away from God without even realizing it. I had lost my passion for God.

Could this be a tragic spiritual reality in your life? Have you lost your passion for God? Is your love growing cold? Do you love Him with the same passion you did when you first met Him as Savior and Lord? This inward connection is very important. We must always understand exactly where we are with God if we are going to experience the ultimate connection, the upward connection with Him.

What happens when we lose our passion for God? First, we lose our love for the things of God. These things just won't be as important as they once were. As we consider what is happening, we rationalize it out of our minds. However, this indicates that we are losing our passion for God.

In time, we will lose our desire to minister to other people. Our desire to meet the needs of others will no longer be important to us. We will justify our actions by blaming our busy schedules. Yet, our life tells us that we are losing our passion for God.

When we lose our passion for God, in time we will lose our desire to win others to Jesus Christ. Sharing our faith with those who don't know Christ will no longer be a priority. We will no longer be willing to sacrifice our time, energy, vision, and money to carry out Jesus' commission for us to go into all the world with the gospel. We will believe Satan's lies that the whole world knows the gospel, so why should we worry about sharing it? The tragic spiritual reality of this type of thinking is that we are losing our passion for God.

When we find ourselves in need of falling in love with Jesus again, what should we do? When we are losing our passion for God, what is the answer? If we have become cold to Christ, what should be our response? There are definite answers to each of these questions. So let's look at . . .

How to Renew Your Passion for God

When we discover that we have a physical problem, we want to do whatever the doctor prescribes for healing. Even if we are told that it may be too late, we still want to do all that we can in order to live. Therefore, once the doctor gives us our prognosis, he provides some steps we must take to cure our physical problem. Usually we can be healed by simply following these steps.

Just as there are steps we must take to be healed physically, there are steps we must take if we want to be healed spiritually. If we want to renew our passion for God, we must follow three essential steps.

We must return to the place where we lost our passion for God and repent. Jesus encouraged the people in the church at Ephesus to return to the place where they had fallen and repent. This is what we must do when we have lost our passion for God.

Usually there is a certain place where our love for Christ began to grow cold. For some it may be when they became angry with someone and failed to resolve that anger. For others, it may have occurred when bitterness crept into their lives over some injustice they suffered. Many have lost their passion for God because they began to neglect their daily devotion to Jesus. Perhaps others have failed to forgive someone who offended them, and this has resulted in their spiritual slide away from loving Jesus. When a person realizes that he has drifted from God, it is important that he determine clearly where he began to lose his passion for Him.

Once we have discovered the event or circumstance that led to our losing our passion for God, we need to respond in repentance. When we have truly repented, we will change our mind about our sin. We will turn from it and do whatever we must do to make things right with God.

Once we have taken this step, we are on our way to having our passion for God renewed. Then there is another step to take.

We need to revitalize our faith in God, in His Word, and in His promises for our lives. The church at Ephesus never came back to Jesus. Their lack of love for Him degenerated into a permanent lifestyle when their faith never became on fire again. Both the church and the city of Ephesus ceased to exist around the 14th century. They lie in ruin to this day.

Once we have gone back to the place or event where we began to lose our passion for God and have repented of it, we need to have our faith revitalized. Our faith has an object; this object is Jesus Christ. If we do not love Him, we will have no faith in Him. That is why we must have our faith revitalized. We need to again become faithful to reading the Word of God. To walk by faith, we must be able to claim the promises contained in His Word.

When we love Jesus, we have a desire to please and obey Him. We do this only as we believe in Him and His Word and obey it. This obedience results in our trusting in His promises.

Once we have followed these two steps, we are ready for the final step. This step is imperative for anyone who wishes to renew his passion for God.

We need to renew our lives with a continual filling of the Holy Spirit. The Bible tells us that we are to be continually filled with the Holy Spirit. This means that we are to live our lives under the Spirit's control. This filling of the Spirit is not a one-time event; instead, it is continuous. Our fellowship with Jesus comes through a constant renewal of the Spirit of God controlling us.

If a person fails to surrender his life, every part of it, to Jesus, then he cannot be filled with the Spirit. This means that we must daily surrender every area of our being to the Holy Spirit's control. We do this by praying a special prayer of commitment to Christ. When we do this, we receive the cleansing power of Jesus' blood for the forgiveness of our sin. We must then surrender each segment of our lives to the Spirit of God. We must give Him our will, our mind, our emotions, our body, our spirit, our motives, our tongue, our attitude, our past, present, and future, our family, our career, and our ministry.

Each of these areas must be daily surrendered to the Spirit's control. If we fail to transfer ownership of these, then we tend to possess them and live in our own power. When we do this, it is only a short time before we lose our passion for Jesus. However, if we yield these areas to Jesus every day and remove our hands from the control of our lives, then our love for Him will remain enthusiastic and strong. The end result is that we are filled with the Spirit of God.

I have learned that it is important for every believer to keep fresh in his mind what Jesus did for him on the cross. By enduring the cross for our sin, Jesus demonstrated a great passion and love for us. He loved us with all He had. He gave us His very life. He died for us.

When we keep in mind what Jesus did for us on the cross, we are more likely to never lose our love for Him. It is more difficult to neglect the Lord in personal devotion when we focus on the fact that He died for us. It is not as easy to disconnect with God when we are reminded daily of His love for us.

Couples often come to me for help because their marriage is falling apart. Many times they come too late for me to help them. Many people avoid seeking counseling because of pride or negligence. Usually it is not the couple who initially comes to my office. Instead, the one who seeks my assistance is the mate who is the most desperate to save the marriage. In fact, this person usually says, "I'm not sure my spouse will even come for counseling." They often continue with the statement, "I'm not sure my spouse would change his (or her) ways if he did come for counseling." This leaves me wondering about each of them.

How Bad Do You Want It?

This is a question we each must consider. As I ask this question, please understand that I am not attempting to judge anyone. I must confess that I am in no position to pass judgment on other people because there have been many times in my Christian walk when I lost my passion for God. However, each time the ultimate question I had to address was whether I really wanted to renew my passion for Him. I had to ask myself if I really wanted things to be like they had once been in my upward connection with God. Only after I answered this question could I expect change to take place. Each time I asked myself, *Ronnie, how bad do you want it?* Once I knew I really desired to renew my passion for Him, regardless of the cost, it happened.

How bad do you want it in your life? How much do you want to have your passion renewed for God? I believe every person can assess this important question better after he addresses three very personal issues.

Will you honestly deal with your sin? The Bible encourages us to deal with our sin. The good news is that when we do, we receive forgiveness. 1 John 1:9 assures us:

If we confess our sins, He is faithful and righteous to forgive us our sins and to cleanse us from all unrighteousness.

In order for a person to experience the depth of Jesus' love, he must receive continual forgiveness of his sins. As we confess our sins, we are agreeing with God, which means we are having His attitude about our sin. We are admitting that our sin deserves judgment. Confession of sin results in forgiveness of and cleansing from our iniquity.

How bad do you want your love for Jesus to be renewed? Do you want it bad enough to deal with the sin that you have been tolerating? Take God's attitude about your sin. Confess it right now and receive forgiveness. This process will become a way of life for any believer who desires to know Jesus in a passionate way.

After you have answered this question, consider . . .

Will you willfully seek to be right with others? Many times our sins hurt other people. Therefore, we must be willing to make things right with others when they have been hurt. Mark 11:25-26 reminds us:

And whenever you stand praying, forgive, if you have anything against anyone; so that your Father also who is in heaven may forgive you your transgressions. But if you do not forgive, neither will your Father who is in heaven forgive your transgressions.

Besides seeking forgiveness from those whom we have wronged, we must be willing to forgive those persons who have offended us. As we do this, we come to understand our Father's forgiveness of our own sins. Therefore, we must aggressively seek to be right with other people. In Romans 12:18 we learn:

If possible, so far as it depends on you, be at peace with all men.

Even in those times when others may not desire to forgive us when we have wronged them, we need to do all we can to be at peace with them.

When our desire is to be right with others, we are wanting our passion for God renewed. This spiritual practice demonstrates a humble spirit. This is the spirit of a Christian who wants his passion for God renewed. Therefore, we must do whatever is necessary to be right with others. We must take the needed steps of action so that our love for Jesus will once again be restored.

This leads us to the final question, which is . . .

Will you seriously surrender to the control of the Holy Spirit? Earlier in this chapter I shared the importance of surrender in every believer's life. Surrendering our lives to the control of the Holy Spirit is essential if we are to renew our passion for God.

We grieve the Holy Spirit when we are filled with emotions toward others that are contrary to the Word of God. We quench the Spirit of God when we disobey any of His Word. However, we are being controlled by the Holy Spirit when we have dealt seriously with our sin, willfully sought to be right with all people, and completely surrendered every area of our lives to His control.

The final result when we are obedient in these areas is that our passion for God is renewed. When this occurs, we discover that we love Jesus just as we did when we first met Him as Savior and Lord. This return to our first love and passion pleases God. As we experience this renewed passion for Jesus, we begin to connect inwardly with who we are. This is necessary if we are to experience the joy of the upward connection with God.

There is still so much to learn about this inward connection. In the next chapter, we will begin to discover . . .

8

Who You Are in Relationship to Who God Is

GOD WAS VERY GOOD when He allowed me to be born into the earthly family that He chose for me. My father and mother reared my brother, sister, and me with much love and care. We always lived in a nice house, and my father enjoyed driving a nice car. My parents provided the best they were able to provide for our family. They never failed to meet my material needs.

More importantly, my parents reared our family in church. Church was the center of our lives, and few times passed when we failed to attend. Not only were we always there for every service and event that took place, but we were even there for the so-called "workdays." Whether we would go to church was never a debatable issue. Even the thought of resisting going to church might have led to an encounter with my dad's thin belt. My parents' greatest priority was to meet the spiritual needs of their children.

I have always been a highly motivated person. Most people who know me well would agree that God has blessed me with various leadership skills. As a young man I felt driven to use these skills in order to be extremely successful. Yet my desire to be successful was not an end in itself. I had a deep need to feel good about myself. To attain that, I thought I had to be successful. Until I was in my mid-twenties, I would do almost anything to achieve success, to feel like I was worth something to others and to God.

It was not until I began work on my doctoral degree that I came to realize that my worth was not based on my being successful. During this time I was spending hours writing my dissertation about biblical stewardship. In this process I discovered some very helpful principles. As I was intensely studying God's doctrine, I began to understand that I receive my worth from God alone. Once I realized this, I began to see who I was as a person. I discovered that it was not my family who could give me my self-worth, even though I was blessed with parents who had provided my every material and spiritual need as a child. My value as a person could only be found in God, and only He could give me a positive feeling of self-worth. I would never be able to find my worth in my own achievements or in how others valued me or my work.

Throughout the years of my ministry I have witnessed several of my mentors fail in their efforts to be true to God. These men were deeply committed to the Lord, but somehow they fell prey to Satan's traps. I used to ponder how this could happen to such devoted men of God, and asked myself, *Why did they fall away from Him?* I sometimes even asked God to help me understand how these people, who had admired Him so much and seemed to love Him deeply, got caught in the traps of Satan.

As I analyzed what had happened to these men, I began to examine their situations in light of the Word of God and in light of my own experience of desiring self-worth. I came to the conclusion that these people never discovered the truth about their worth. Many had attempted to attain their worth in the wrong places and ended up feeling empty. They then became open to Satan's attacks and became one of his victims. These people had failed to discover who they were in relationship to who God is.

My primary goal in life is to finish well the race that God has set before me. I do not want to become exhausted before the race is concluded. I do not want to embarrass my Lord, my family, or my church. However, I believe there is a connection between a person's completing the race well and knowing who he is in relationship to who God is.

It is obvious that many Christians, including church leaders, have a major problem. I know many fine believers who have the same problem that I had until I was in my mid-twenties. It is also the same dilemma with which many of my mentors struggled and which resulted in their falling away from God. This problem causes a disruption in numerous relationships. Satan has used this to ruin many lives.

The problem is identity. It surfaces when a person finds himself wondering, *Where can I find my worth?* Too many people simply do not know who they are, much less where they are going in this life. Countless families have become fragmented due to this problem. Our young people are being reared in this complex fragmented society. The only solution to the problem of identity is for a person to discover who he is in relationship to who God is.

When people do not have an understanding of who they are, then their lives represent the fragmented society in which we live. This is why we see so much disorder and confusion in the lives of many Christians. They are often unbalanced and go from one extreme to another. The result is a powerless spiritual life. They spend their time searching for their identity, and in the process are disconnected from God.

When we are disconnected from our Creator, we will never discover our worth. Only as we have an upward connection with God will we learn of our worth by inwardly connecting with ourselves. We can forever seek our identity but never find it, unless we discover who we are in relationship to who God is. This is our only hope of finishing our race victoriously.

Do you desire a life of order? Do you want to live a balanced life? Do you want to discover your identity? Would you like to experience God's power? The only way this will happen is by learning who you are in relationship to who God is. Therefore, will you join with me in this adventure over the next few pages?

To solve the quest for identity, we must consider five important words. This may seem like a simplistic approach, but I believe the answer is very simple. I also believe it can be found by applying these five concepts to the search for who we are in relationship to who God is.

Manager

When I became pastor of First Baptist Church in Palacios, Texas, in 1981, the chairman of the Pastor Search Committee was a man named Billy Hamlin. Billy was the owner of an affiliated food store in that small town of just under five thousand people. He was the first person I had ever watched manage a business.

Billy worked long hours every day and was there when the doors finally closed at night. He was not afraid of work, nor was any task too menial for him. Billy could be found doing anything from handing out payroll checks to sacking groceries and even delivering groceries to various people in town. He often said to me, "Pastor, great day, great day . . . the doors are swinging, cash registers ringing, and Billy's singing." Frankly, Billy couldn't sing at all.

As I watched Billy, I learned what a manager does. A manager constantly inspects the store. He insists on quality work from every employee. The manager takes care of anything that must be done and is committed to making the store a success.

When we examine God's Word to consider who He is and our relationship to Him, we further learn about the concept of being a manager. In Genesis 1:26-28 we find:

Then God said, "Let Us make man in Our image, according to Our likeness; and let them rule over the fish of the sea and over the birds of the sky and over the cattle and over all the earth, and over every creeping thing that creeps on the earth." And God created man in His own image, in the image of God He created him; male and female He created them. And God blessed them; and God said to them, "Be fruitful and multiply, and fill the earth, and subdue it; and rule over the fish of the sea and over the birds of the sky, and over every living thing that moves on the earth."

This passage gives us one of the most important words in Scripture that tells us who we are in relationship to who God is.

The key word is "rule." This word is used twice in these verses. It comes from the Hebrew word *radah*, which means "I rule" or "I have dominion" on the earth. We get our word for stewardship from this word.

We discover this same principle in several passages in the New Testament. One of these is found in Luke 16:2, which states:

And he called him and said to him, "What is this I hear about you? Give an account of your stewardship, for you can no longer be steward."

The key word here is "stewardship." It comes from the Greek word *oikonomos*, which means "a manager of an estate" or "an inspector of goods."

The words "rule" and "stewardship" mean the same thing. They reveal who we are in relationship to who God is.

In the third chapter of this book we considered the fact that God is sovereign. We know that God owns all, has all, is all, and demands our all. He is a great God!

When we synthesize each of these ideas into one major thought, we learn something incredible about our worth. Since God owns everything, He has placed us as managers over His creation. Our job is to look after His estate. We are to rule over His creation. Therefore, we have worth as managers based upon who God is, owner of everything.

God wants us to manage our personal lives in a way that honors Him. He wants us to rule over His possessions that He has entrusted to our care. God desires us to manage over the wealth that He has given to us.

When we realize who we are based upon who God is, we discover that we are to be managers over His creation. God believes we have worth, or He would never have given us this responsibility. He expects us to look after all of His affairs on earth. These affairs are comprehensive since God owns everything.

Our identity problem begins to diminish when we fulfill God's will for our lives by being a manager over all that He has entrusted to us. We realize our worth when we know that God is depending on us to manage well the things He has given us. I am motivated to finish the race well when I understand that God has appointed me as a manager over His creation. Therefore, I have worth based upon who God is. I am thankful that my value is not found in any other place or any person.

This is only the beginning of our understanding of who we are based upon who God is. We must now discover that God believes we are . . .

Special

My wife, Jeana, does a splendid job of making me feel special. She loves being a housewife and mother. Jeana is motivated to meet my needs and the needs of our children. Occasionally she leaves a card for me just to remind me of her love. Every Valentine's Day she bakes a red velvet cake in the shape of a heart just for me. Jeana constantly runs errands and takes care of details so I do not have to bother with them. As I consider the many things she does for me, I truly feel special.

Recently Jeana arranged to "kidnap" me and take me away to a beautiful secluded log cabin. She had spent much time and thought in planning this time together, and it was wonderful. During this short get-away, Jeana had planned every detail for one reason: more than anything, she wanted to make me feel special. In doing so, she showed her love for me.

One day Jesus had a long conversation with a group of people who had gathered at the Mount of Olives. He began to share with them some principles for successful living. During this time, Jesus spoke on the issue of human worth. In Matthew 6:26 He said:

Look at the birds of the air, that they do not sow, neither do they reap, nor gather into barns, and yet your heavenly Father feeds them. Are you not worth much more than they?

This passage tells us just how much Jesus wanted us to understand where our worth is found. At the same time that He speaks about our worth, Jesus also talks about the role of our heavenly Father.

The Lord continued to share in this passage how special we are to God. Matthew 6:30 states:

But if God so arrays the grass of the field, which is alive today and tomorrow is thrown into the furnace, will He not much more do so for you, O men of little faith?

Jesus is telling us just how special we are to Him. He says that we are special because the Father will meet our needs. Just as God makes us feel special by meeting our needs, we make others feel special by meeting their needs.

Do you really want to know who you are in relationship to who God is? You are special! Because of God's loving care for us, He meets our needs. Therefore, we are special to God.

People may tell us that we have no value. Satan may point the world to us and yell in unison with them, "You are losers!" At times our media can be heard suggesting that evangelical Christians are "ignorant fundamentalists." In so doing, they are trying to equate us with the radical fundamentalist groups in the world. Nevertheless, God says we are special.

As a matter of fact, we are so special that God left heaven and came to earth in the form of man. He thought we are so special that He wanted us to live with Him forever in heaven. This is why Jesus died for us. We are special to God because of the finished work of Jesus Christ.

Many people tell us that we are special only if we are successful according to this world's standards. However, our worth is never based on our performance. Our worth is based on what God says about us, and He says that we are special.

It is easy for a person to seek his worth by attaining various goals that he determines are important. Many people set quotas that we must meet and suggest that we are great only if we meet these quotas. The fallacy in this thinking is that it suggests that if we fail in this area, we have no worth. Again, we must remember that we will never find our worth based on our performance, because while at times we may perform well, occasionally we will not. Our worth is not based on good performance; it is based on who God says we are. He says we are special!

Many people suggest that we have worth only if we are liked by others. It is dangerous to attempt to gain worth from the mere approval of others. What others think of us can never be the dominant factor in our feeling special. Due to the fallen nature of man, there is no way people will always give us their approval. Therefore, our worth is not based on what others think about us. It is based only on what God says. He says we are special!

As we understand who we are in relationship to who God is, we know we have worth. How do we know this? We know this because God has made us managers over all that He has entrusted to us. We are special! What else do we learn about who we are in relationship to who God is? Our next key word is . . .

Fellowship

When I gave my life to Jesus Christ, I entered into a relationship with Him. The Christian life is a relationship with God through Jesus Christ. Once that relationship is established, it is developed through fellowship. Fellowship with God travels on the tracks of a relationship. As I spend time with Him, developing our relationship, I have the privilege of experiencing fellowship with God. This fellowship is one of the great privileges of being a Christian.

When I come to understand who I am in relationship to who God is, I am able to comprehend that God wants to fellowship with me. He assures us in 1 John 1:3 that:

What we have seen and heard we proclaim to you also, that you may have fellowship with us; and indeed our fellowship is with the Father, and with His Son Jesus Christ.

The key word in this passage is "fellowship." It comes from the Greek word *koinonia,* which means to set aside one's private interests and desires to join in with another person for a common purpose. God wants us to set aside our own agendas and join in fellowship with Him.

It is important for us to understand that the great God of this universe wants to have fellowship with us. When we consider this fact, we are humbled. God wants to know us. He wants to share in our lives. Because He thinks we are very important, God wants to fellowship with us.

When we meditate on this privilege, we realize that we are very blessed. We are blessed to have the joy of sharing in the life of Jesus Christ. This is who we are in Christ. We are also fortunate to be able to experience fellowship with God. We have a personal relationship with our Creator. The Apostle Paul stated the following in Philippians 3:10:

That I may know Him, and the power of His resurrection and the fellowship of His sufferings, being conformed to His death.

When we share in the sufferings of Jesus Christ, we get to know Him. Through knowing Him, we are able to experience the same power that raised Jesus from the dead.

This personal experience of fellowship depicts the power of discovering who we are in relationship to who God is. He is personal and interested in every detail of our lives. What a God!

Therefore, as a manager of all that God has entrusted to us, we have worth to God. He considers us so special that He wants to fellowship with us. He gave His life for us in order to make this possible.

As we continue to grow in our understanding of who we are in relationship to who God is, there is another word we must consider. This word is . . .

Accountability

When I was a boy, we lived in a large two-story house located on a beautiful piece of property. The house was surrounded by trees, and the lawn was very big. The yard work was always a challenge because there was so much to do. As I got older it became my responsibility to mow the lawn. Dad would always tell me the day when I was to mow. He would remind me to "be sure to have the lawn mowed by the time I come home from work this afternoon."

I always began this chore with good intentions. All too frequently, though, the lawn mower would break or would fail to start after I quit for a few minutes to get a drink of water. While I waited for the mower to cooperate with me, I often wandered off and got involved in play with my friends. In no time at all, I would look up to discover that my dad was turning into the driveway. He could quickly see that I had not completed my job. His first question was always, "Why haven't you finished mowing the lawn?" I would try to explain that I couldn't get the lawn mower to start. Dad would then march over to the mower and pull the cord. It would start on the first try.

My day of reckoning finally came. I knew I was in big trouble. Dad had warned me not to let this happen again. But it did. He used his slim belt on my back side. I quickly learned what it means to be accountable.

If I want to understand who I am in relationship to who God is, I must learn the concept of accountability. In Romans 14:12 we read:

So then each one of us shall give account of himself to God.

The word accountability comes from the Greek word *logon*, which means to give a word-by-word accounting to God. This is a critical concept that we must grasp.

When we understand that God wants to make us accountable to Him, we understand that He loves us. Just as my father made me accountable in order to teach me the importance of responsibility and follow-through, God wants us to be reminded that we will one day stand before Him. At that time we will be accountable to Him for how we lived our lives. God will hold us accountable only because He loves us.

We need accountability in every area of our lives. We must be accountable for our families. We need to be accountable for our jobs. We need to be accountable in our spiritual lives. Accountability has a way of calling us to a new level of commitment. This new level of commitment is to the God who loves us enough to make us accountable.

We have learned so much about who we are in relationship to who God is. However, one concept remains that is necessary to make this understanding complete. This word is . . .

Desire

A person can know in many ways that he is a Christian. One of the primary ways we can know that Jesus is in our lives is by our desire or hunger to know Him. Before I knew Christ, my greatest desire was to be accepted by others. I sought this acceptance by trying to perform well on a football field. I devoted all my efforts to accomplishing this selfish goal. However, when I met Jesus as Savior and Lord, I began to have a hunger only to please Him. My greatest desire was to know Jesus and to serve Him. I could not get enough of Him and enough of serving Him.

I came to realize that as a Christian manager of all that God has entrusted to me, I am special to God. I am able to have fellowship with Him daily. He loves me enough to make me accountable in my relationship to Him. Therefore, what should I give back to Him for being such a great God to me? Desire! A desire that motivates me . . .

To honor God in every area of my life. One of the greatest challenges in my relationship with my wife is to honor her. Honoring Jeana means that I regard her as being very valuable to me. I give her high esteem.

As I understand who I am in relationship to who God is, I will honor Him with my life. This means that I will esteem Him as valuable to my life. The Bible says in 1 Samuel 2:30:

Therefore the Lord God of Israel declares, "I did indeed say that your house and the house of your father should walk before Me forever"; but now the Lord declares, "Far be it from Me—for those who honor Me I will honor, and those who despise Me will be lightly esteemed."

This Scripture teaches us that if we honor God, He will honor us. Once again, we see a great feature about God. He promises blessings to us as we honor Him.

Are you honoring God in your life? Are you esteeming Him as being valuable to you? When we understand fully who we are in Him, we will honor Him with our lives. Our desire must be to honor God with everything that He has given us and with our whole being.

Not only must our desire be to honor God, but our desire must also be . . .

To bring glory to God. When we mature in the Lord, we put off our old desires of selfish gain. At the same time, we come to desire to bring glory to God and to Him alone. In 1 Corinthians 10:31 we read:

Whether, then, you eat or drink or whatever you do, do all to the glory of God.

We are to bring glory to God with all that we have and with all that we are. This means that when we experience any type of success, we give all the glory to God. It means that when we experience any kind of failure, we still give all the glory to God. So in everything that we say or do, it is to be done to the glory of God. This is our highest offer of praise to Him.

What I have shared in this chapter pertains to who we are in relationship to who God is. We have considered what we are to be with the great God who desires to connect with us. This will occur when we experience the inward connection of understanding who we are. We cannot learn this in a self-esteem seminar. We cannot discover this in a success magazine. We only learn who we are as we understand who God is.

We do not have to live with an identity crisis. We have worth. We are valuable to God. Therefore, our lives can be orderly, balanced, and full of spiritual power. This is our only hope of finishing well the race of life.

We have already learned that God desires to connect with us. However . . .

9

Are You Desperate to Reconnect with God?

THE DAY AFTER WE DIS-
covered that Jeana had cancer, we went to see an oncologist. He painted a hopeful but honest picture of Jeana's condition. However, he told us that only through surgery could he accurately know her true prognosis.

Exactly one week after learning of Jeana's cancer, we traveled to Houston to visit M. D. Anderson Hospital. I made arrangements for us to stay in a special room in a lovely hotel. In spite of the wonderful accommodations, though, the night seemed so long.

The next morning my parents arrived at our hotel to take us to the hospital. On the way there I detoured to a Christian bookstore where I purchased a tape for my mother. As we drove toward the huge medical center, where I had visited on many occasions as a pastor, I felt as though I was gasping for air. Quietness filled my parents' Suburban as the next song on the new tape began to play. My mind and heart were encouraged with the lyrics, "our God reigns." My fears withdrew for a moment. God had answered my prayer; He was with us.

The lobby of a cancer hospital is like no other. People of all ages are present, using wheelchairs or walkers or walking on their own. Many are without hair; most are without hope. There is no laughter. Pain permeates the room. The worst kind of pain is not physical; it is the fear of the unknown.

The breast surgeon met with us and affirmed Jeana's condition. He answered all of our questions and shared about the horrifying chemotherapy that loomed before us. The physician assured us that he would be in contact with Dr. Kendrick. He asked me to call him from the airport, at which time he would be able to tell us the grade of Jeana's cancer. This report would determine her future treatment.

While waiting to board our flight home, I called the doctor. He informed me that Jeana had what is called "nuclear grade one cancer." I learned that this cancer is the worst kind, which is apparent from the adjectives used to describe it: mean, angry, and aggressive.

Jeana cried all the way home. Reality had come. She had cancer. I attempted to comfort her, but, needless to say, I needed my own comfort.

I was desperate to reconnect with God. This physical interruption moved me toward God, desperate for Him to move supernaturally in our situation.

On Wednesday morning, nine days after the initial shock, I got up early and shared the following with God in my prayer journal:

Faith comes by hearing and hearing by the Word. We need a word today about Jeana's health. I must hear from you by surgery tomorrow or else, Lord, there will be no faith. I commit, due to feeling inspired, to pray and fast until after surgery.

God honored my fasting. He honored my connecting with Him in prayer. He spoke very clearly to me from the book of Isaiah. I read the passage in Isaiah 43:1-3:

Do not fear, for I have redeemed you; I have called you by name; you are Mine! When you pass through the waters, I will be with you; And through the rivers, they will not overflow you. When you walk through the fire, you will not be scorched, Nor will the flame burn you. For I am the Lord your God, the Holy One of Israel, your Savior.

I had what I needed to be filled with faith. God had spoken to me in my desperation to reconnect with Him.

Subsequent to her major surgery, Jeana underwent two minor surgeries to prepare her for the treatment that was to follow. She went through six weeks of radiation. Then she received over six months of very strong chemotherapy. During these months I watched her physical appearance change. She lost all of her hair. The Lord used this to keep us before Him in fasting and prayer one day each week. God honored our desperation to reconnect with Him through our submitting to this biblical principle.

Most people know very little about personal sacrifice today. Personal sacrifice is when a person has to give up something, which may even be painful, in order to reconnect with God. It may also be when a person has to give up someone or something that he loves very much, in order to reconnect with Him. The principle of fasting and prayer involves personal sacrifice.

We have idolized the word "commitment" in the Christian life. However, I believe the key word that is found in the life of the believer who is controlled by the Holy Spirit is "surrender." When we surrender our lives to Him, we are indicating our willingness to endure personal sacrifice. Our level of surrender and personal sacrifice determines the depth of our walk with God.

Few Christians practice the principle of fasting and prayer. The reason for this may be ignorance rather than disobedience. However, when life seems to be falling in around us and God is our only hope and deliverance, our willingness to practice God's principles in order to obtain a supernatural power changes. It all depends on our level of desperation.

Fasting involves abstinence. This abstinence should be done with a spiritual goal in mind. When a person fasts, he abstains from food and water. Fasting also is done by abstaining only from food. Another form of fasting involves abstaining from sex, when the marriage partners agree. A fast usually lasts for 24 hours, unless the person feels led of God to honor Him with an extended fast. I usually practice fasting from sunset one day until sunset the next day.

It is important to remember that fasting is to be coupled with a spiritual goal in mind. For example, during the year of Jeana's cancer and the treatment that followed, my goal for fasting and prayer each week was for her physical healing. There are times when my goal for fasting and prayer is singular. At other times, I may have up to three major burdens for which I feel led to bring to the Lord through this commitment.

I believe that desperation is the major factor that determines when a Christian should honor the principle of prayer and fasting. Desperation leads to a willingness to endure sacrifice. Fasting and prayer involves personal sacrifice. Therefore, the question we must answer is, "Are we desperate to reconnect with God?"

Scripture gives us insight to five occasions when we are to fast and pray. The first one is . . .

When We Are Desperate for God

Numerous times I have been desperate to reconnect with God. I knew that things were not quite right with Him, so I fasted and prayed. At times when I have realized that I needed a fresh anointing of the Holy Spirit upon my pulpit ministry, I have practiced this biblical principle. There have also been times when I just felt compelled to draw near to God; I fasted and prayed.

Jesus was desperate to be in the Father's presence, so He regularly fasted and prayed. In his first major attack from Satan during His public ministry, Jesus fasted and prayed. In Matthew 4:1-2 we read:

Then Jesus was led up by the Spirit into the wilderness to be tempted by the devil. And after He had fasted forty days and nights, He then became hungry.

Jesus was desperate to be in the solitude of His Father's presence, so He had fasted and prayed for forty days and nights.

We read a great deal about Moses and his role as leader to the children of Israel in the Old Testament. What a challenge was set before him! On many occasions Moses became desperate for God. Exodus 34:28 records the following about one of these moments of Moses' desperation:

So he was there with the Lord forty days and forty nights; he did not eat bread or drink water. And he wrote on the tablets the words of the covenant, the Ten Commandments.

As a result of his fasting and prayer, Moses reconnected with God. In this fellowship experience, God gave to Moses the Ten Commandments. But Moses was desperate for God and he reconnected with Him.

The prophet Joel provides another illustration of a person who was desperate for God to move in his life, as well as among the people of God. In Joel 1:14 the Bible says:

Consecrate a fast, proclaim a solemn assembly; gather the elders and all the inhabitants of the land to the house of the Lord your God, and cry out to the Lord.

Joel wanted God's people to be able to call out successfully to the Lord. He was desperate for them to be connected with Him. Therefore, Joel called the people of God to a fast. This action was coupled with prayer. As a result, the people saw God move among them.

Are we desperate enough for God to surrender our will and desires in order to fast and pray? Are we desperate enough for His power that we would be willing to fast and pray for 24 hours?

When we feel we just need to be with God, fasting and prayer can give us the entree we need to experience Him in the fullness of that upward connection. When we need to hear God's voice, fasting and prayer can give us a special sensitivity to Him. When we are desperate for God, we should fast and pray. When else should we do this?

When We Are Desperate to Be Right with God

Times have come in my spiritual life when I felt that my number one need was to become clean before God. I sensed that, for some reason, I had disconnected from Him and had begun to tolerate various sins in my life. When I became aware of my condition, I realized I had a choice to make. Either I would continue in my slide away from God, or I could fast and pray as I examined myself to get things right with Him.

King David is a wonderful example of a person who became desperate to get right with God. He was supposed to be away in battle as the king. Yet he neglected this responsibility. While walking on his roof one night, David noticed a woman bathing. He was enticed by her beauty and lusted after her. The king sent for this woman and eventually committed sexual adultery with her. He then tried to cover up his sin and even arranged for Bathsheba's husband to be killed while he was on the front line of battle. David later learned that Bathsheba was pregnant with his child. God used Nathan, the prophet, to inform David that he had sinned against God. A boy was born to Bathsheba, but he became very ill. We read of David's response to his son's sickness in 2 Samuel 12:15-16:

So Nathan went to his house. Then the Lord struck the child that Uriah's widow bore to David, so that he was very sick. David therefore inquired of God for the child; and David fasted and went and lay all night on the ground.

Why did David fast and pray? Was it for the child's healing?

David had walked with God long enough that he was aware that he had sinned against God. He realized that God was judging his sin through the child's illness and eventual death. David fasted and prayed in order to get his own life right with God. He had become disconnected from God and had fallen deep into sin. The king fasted and prayed so he would be able to again sense the power of God in his life.

David practiced this biblical principle on several occasions. In Psalm 69:10 we read:

When I wept in my soul with fasting, it became my reproach.

David's brokenness had led him to fasting and praying. He wanted to examine himself and be right with God.

There are many times when we all need to examine ourselves spiritually. Times come when we need to know we are right with the Lord. Often the only way we can gain power over a particular sin and its guilt is by fasting and praying. When we realize that sin has crept into our lives, we should fast and pray. This response will give us a special sensitivity to God's Spirit so that He can reveal our sin to us. In this process, He will also supply the power to overcome the sin that entangles us. God does not want us to be in bondage to sin. Fasting and prayer leads to the dynamic spiritual freedom from sin that He desires us to experience.

The Lord wants us to be continually connected with Him. When we feel disconnected, prayer and fasting may be the answer we need. If we become desperate enough to examine ourselves and be right with God, we should fast and pray.

When is another time that prayer and fasting is appropriate?

When We Are Desperate for God's Direction

There have been times when I felt that God was wanting to redirect my path. For some reason God seems to permit a spirit of restlessness to come over a person when He desires to change their direction. As I have experienced this restlessness, I have sensed the need to know where God was leading me, both personally as well as in my ministry. On several occasions when I have been desperate for His direction, I have fasted and prayed. As I did so, He has often reaffirmed that I was in the correct place of ministry. However, on a few of these occasions, God has led me into a new ministry.

As a leader of God's people, when I need specific clarity about the Lord's direction for our church, I often fast and pray. When I do this, I usually write in my spiritual journal what I am asking God's direction about during the particular time of fasting. The direction may involve a decision concerning staff, a specific area of ministry, or the entire membership. We all need to know what God desires to do with us and where He wants us to go. When I sense this need and am desperate to know His direction, I pray and fast.

Daniel, the prophet, was desperate for God to reveal to him the direction for the children of Israel. They were in the middle of their captivity when Daniel became desperate to know how much longer they would be in bondage. In Daniel 9:3 we read:

So I gave my attention to the Lord God to seek Him by prayer and supplications, with fasting, sackcloth, and ashes.

Daniel wanted to know God's direction for his own life as well as for the people of God. Therefore, he fasted and prayed. As always, God honored these actions and revealed His direction to Daniel.

Most Christians are so busy with life that they do not spend time considering what God may want them to do in a specific area of life. This need for direction may pertain to a purchase, a career choice, a new job, a business decision, the choice of a mate, or an action that may be needed. The average Christian does not even seek God's direction in these instances. He simply does what he feels is the best thing to do at the time. This kind of decision making often leads to wrong decisions. In spite of the interruptions and pressures we may face, we need to take the time to know God's direction in every area of our lives.

The way we can discover His direction is through prayer and fasting. This is God's way of getting us ready to sense Him and to know His will for us. As believers we do not have to live a roller coaster ride as we attempt to determine God's plan for us. If we are desperate to know His will regarding a particular area of our lives, then we need to practice the principle of fasting and prayer until God clearly reveals His direction to us.

If we are desperate to reconnect with God, then we should be willing to follow this principle that will enable us to do so. Another occasion when we should practice fasting and prayer is . . .

When We Are Desperate About Our Nation's Spiritual Condition

We are witnessing a rapid moral decline in America. The family unit's fragmentation and degeneration are the major reasons for this decline. Some of the secular liberal media are even trying to redefine the concept of family to include the marriages of homosexuals. We have recently seen much of the progress that had been made to stop abortions in our country come to an end. It now appears that abortions are here to stay. We are even hearing of assisted suicides, and people justify this action with the idea of our right to "quality of life."

This moral decline in America is now infiltrating our churches. Many denominations are having to address issues that they have never had to address. Adultery, sexual abuse, and homosexuality are issues that many churches are having to confront, not just in their membership but in their leadership. These are indeed days of rapid moral decline.

What should be our response? If we are desperate about the condition of our country, the only answer is fasting and prayer. Years ago the people of God were surrounded by their enemies. Everywhere they looked, the forecast was gloomy. Jehoshaphat, their leader, decided to respond in a godly manner. His response is given in 2 Chronicles 20:3:

And Jehoshaphat was afraid and turned his attention to seek the Lord, and proclaimed a fast throughout all Judah.

Therefore, Judah observed a fast and saw the hand of God move in their situation. What did God do?

First, God confused the enemy. They turned on each other so that God's people were spared. This was a miracle of God. Why did it happen? Because God's people fasted and prayed.

We see the same kind of miracle take place in the city of Nineveh. God was going to bring judgment upon this entire city. Jonah 3:5 records the following:

Then the people of Nineveh believed in God; and they called a fast and put on sackcloth from the greatest to the least of them.

Jonah was not excited about being God's prophet in Nineveh. However, in spite of Jonah's attitude, God used him. When the Lord saw the hearts of the people turn toward Him, He dismissed from His mind the calamity of judgment He had planned for them. As a result, Nineveh did not experience judgment at this particular time; instead, it experienced spiritual revival. This revival took place because of God's people who had fasted and prayed.

I have never seen the desperation level for God to do something in our country as high in America as it is at this time. I believe that the intensity of our becoming desperate for God to step into our situation and do something is growing every day.

We do not need to be deceived by Satan, even in our political process. Even though we need to be involved in political activities as much as possible, this is not the solution to our dilemma. The answer for America's problems will come only from a great moving of God. The rapid pace of our moral decline calls us to days of fasting and praying with our goal being that God would bring revival to America.

The Christian response to the condition of America should not be negative conversations at the local coffeeshop. Our response should be to fast and pray. I am encouraged by the growth of the prayer movement we are seeing all across our land. God is raising up many churches with a great commitment to prayer. These churches need to expand this commitment by adding the principle of fasting to their prayer ministries. The response would be incredible.

I believe America is in the condition it is in because most churches in our country are dead. They are dead because most of the believers in these churches are not really daily connected with

God. The church needs revival! America will not change until revival comes to the church. However, revival will not come without a commitment to fasting and prayer.

Are we desperate enough about the spiritual condition of America that we are willing to pray and fast? The hope for our country is not in the person who occupies the White House or the Congress. Our hope lies only in spiritual awakening. This could come when God's people begin to fast and pray for our country's spiritual condition. Are we desperate for our country to reconnect with God?

One other occasion when we should fast and pray is . . .

When We Are Desperate to Succeed

We live in a country that is dominated by a success mentality. This drive for success is embraced by almost every segment of our society. We are told that success is dependent on what we wear, our skills, and even on the people we know who can help us. Success by itself is not a worthwhile goal; however, success that comes as the result of obeying God's principles is a worthwhile goal to have in every area of our lives.

When Nehemiah was told about the condition of Jerusalem, he was broken-hearted. He wept when he heard that the walls of this city had been destroyed. God gave Nehemiah a burden to be the man whom He would use to rebuild the walls. We read about his burden in Nehemiah 1:4, which says:

Now it came about when I heard these words, I sat down and wept and mourned for days; and I was fasting and praying before the God of heaven.

In the midst of Nehemiah's fasting and praying, he learned that God had given him such a heavy burden because God wanted to use him to rebuild the walls of Jerusalem. A miracle happened. Nehemiah returned to Jerusalem and was able to stand against fierce opposition. God used him the way He had intended to rebuild these walls. God had assigned Nehemiah with a job to do. As the result of his prayer and fasting, Nehemiah experienced great success in performing the work God had assigned him.

Fasting and prayer also played an important role in the New Testament church at Antioch. The Bible says in Acts 13:2-3:

And while they were ministering to the Lord and fasting, the Holy Spirit said, "Set apart for Me Barnabas and Saul for the work to which I have called them." Then, when they had fasted and prayed and laid their hands on them, they sent them away.

God assigned to the church at Antioch the same task that He has assigned to every church today. That task is to win the world to Jesus Christ. This church was faced with the tremendous challenge of making a difference for Christ. They were commissioned to take the gospel across the world. Fasting and prayer fit into their God-given assignment.

We will be successful in whatever God has called us to do if prayer and fasting are a part of it. The church can even penetrate the pagan culture of our day if we pray and fast as a part of our strategy to reach its city for Jesus. So regardless of our assignment as a believer, we will experience success when we involve God through fasting and prayer.

I call this the God factor. When He is factored into our personal lives, we will see the miracle working power of God. When He is factored into our churches, we will see them once again penetrating our cities for Christ. All of this depends on whether or not we are desperate enough to want to reconnect with God.

The ministry of prayer is the most important ministry in the church where I serve as pastor. Through the years our conviction in wanting God involved at every level of activity has grown. His involvement is obtained only through prayer. Even though the way we have accomplished our prayer ministry has changed over time, we believe in the power of the God connection. We now have over seven hundred people who pray for one hour each week for the ministries of our church. Each month we provide them with a specially designed prayer guide that lists up to 25 areas of our church's ministries that we want them to pray for during that specific month. We provide them with a Scripture promise to claim along with each prayer request. Then we inform them of the specific requests for prayer for each item. This means that during each hour of the day several people are praying at the same time, in the same way, and for the same requests. This is power!

We recently held a special week-long evangelistic crusade at our church. Five months prior to this event, these seven hundred prayer warriors began to pray for a great harvest of souls. This means that for five months our people were praying around the clock for this crusade.

Forty days prior to this event, I asked these same people, as well as any other persons in our church who wished to join us, to commit to fasting one day each week. So for 40 days and nights our church was involved in fasting and praying for this evangelistic crusade. Our fast ended on the day that the event began.

During these 40 days we were asking God to allow us to reach one thousand people for Christ. God honored our commitment to fasting and prayer in a miraculous way!

During this week in which we attacked our area with the gospel, we saw 2,625 people come to Christ during the public invitations. These were people we were able to obtain information on, talk with, and encourage in their new-found faith in Christ. During this week, over four hundred of these people were baptized in our church. Over 32,000 persons attended this event, even though our city has a population of less than 30,000. What makes the results of this crusade even more incredible is the fact that one of the largest snowfalls in our area's history took place during this week. The snowfall ranged from 10 to 18 inches throughout our region. I believe God permitted this unusual weather so that He alone would be able to receive the glory for what He was going to do among His people.

Can man's efforts accomplish this kind of success? Absolutely not! God stepped in because His people had fasted and prayed for Him to impact our area with the gospel of Jesus Christ. When God gets involved, we begin to operate in a new dimension. God can do more in a moment than we can do in a lifetime. Only the Lord God can receive the glory for the dynamic impact that was made upon our region.

Our people were desperate for God to move in a major spiritual manner. We demonstrated this desperation through fasting and prayer. We were willing to live according to His ways rather than our own. God honored this desire to reconnect with Him, so that we could experience the power of the upward connection.

How desperate are you to reconnect with God? How desperate are you for Him? How desperate are you for God's direction? How desperate are you to see Him bring spiritual awakening to our country? How desperate are you to succeed in the tasks God has assigned to you? Your level of desperation will determine your surrender to the powerful spiritual principle of fasting and prayer.

The power of the inward connection takes place when we are willing to look honestly at ourselves like Isaiah did. This inward connection comes alive when we renew our passion for God. It moves to another level when we begin to see ourselves as God sees us. This inward connection supercedes all of our expectations once we are willing to sacrifice personally and practice the principle of fasting and prayer. When this inward connection takes place fully in our lives, we begin to live in the power of being upwardly connected with God.

How do we reconnect with God? We begin to reconnect with Him by looking upward and reuniting with Him in the power of that upward connection. We continue this reconnection by looking inwardly and discovering the power of the inward connection. When we are reconnected with God and with ourselves, we are then ready to move toward the fulfillment of . . .

The outward connection.

Part Three

The
Outward
Connection

10

Your Life Never Lies to You

My LIFE HAS NEVER LIED
to me. My priorities have been revealed in every decision I have
ever made. There have been times when my decisions have con-
tradicted what I claimed were my convictions. During those times
I have tried to justify, at least to myself, the decisions I have made.
As my spiritual life has matured, I have learned that my life
always mirrors my priorities. My life never lies to me.

I have always felt that my family should be of greater importance to me than my ministry to the local church. After my sons
were born, though, I came to realize that this belief was only an
intellectual one. The reality of my life did not demonstrate what I
believed. Through my years of ministry I became aware of how
important my family was to me. I began to see that the church
could dismiss me tomorrow, but my family would need me as long
as I live. Therefore, I realized that I needed to realign my life
practically to reflect what I believed intellectually.

I had to ask myself some very piercing questions: *Did I want to
attend meetings every night at the church, or did I want to be with my
family? Did I want to be gone from home constantly in order to preach
at meetings all across our country, or did I want to see my children grow
up? Did I want to work seven days a week for the rest of my life, or did*

I want to commit to spending one day a week with my wife in order for us to have a wonderful relationship? Did I have a greater desire to be a good golfer than I had to be a good father?

As I considered these questions, I determined that I wanted to get my priorities in the right order.

I have always had a difficult time mastering what I call "the shuffle." The shuffle is when I attempt to be a good pastor, a good father, a good husband, a good friend, and a good leader, all at the same time. Being successful in each of these areas is an astounding challenge. Each of these areas cries out for attention, simultaneously. Therefore, they can cause a person to feel a great deal of stress and even guilt, especially when there is the feeling that none of them have been given the attention that is needed.

When my wife was diagnosed with cancer, my commitment to the right priorities was reinforced. The moment the doctor told me of her illness, nothing else mattered to me except Jeana's health. The church was no longer so important to me. Other matters that had been of great concern now seemed trivial. Events in the news or the outcome of sporting events really didn't matter anymore. As God used this experience to readjust my priorities, He permanently etched in my mind and my heart that God and family are to be the major priorities in life.

The outward connection in our lives is when we are challenged to relate well to everyone and everything. This outward connection is fulfilled when we have a proper relationship with the persons and things to which we are to relate. The only way this goal can be accomplished is when we are reconnected with God and are experiencing the inward connection of knowing who we are in relationship to who God is. When the upward and inward connections are in order, we will be effective in connecting outwardly with those persons and things that we are to relate to in life.

This process involves decision-making. In fact, the decisions we make reflect our priorities. Therefore, only as we have the right priorities will we keep from being distracted by the shuffle's challenge. At times our goal may simply be to survive; however, our real goal should be to experience spiritual power. We will never have spiritual power without the right priorities.

Three truths that we must never forget are:

- *Every decision we make mirrors our priorities.*
- *Wrong priorities will result in bad decisions.*
- *Bad decisions hurt us as well as everyone around us.*

These facts are true for every person. When we ignore these truths, we experience frustration and disorder.

For example, John had been working all week. His schedule had left him no time for his family. As he came home at the end of this hectic week, his wife reminded him of two events that he needed to attend with his children on Saturday morning. She also informed John that she wanted the family to eat lunch out that day so they could spend some special time together.

Just as John learned of his family's plans for the weekend, he received a call from a friend who wanted him to play golf. Because John had worked so hard all week, felt exhausted, and believed he had earned the right to some personal time, he agreed to meet his friend for golf. As he hung up the phone, his wife asked, "Who was that?" John cowardly informed her that he had to play golf with his friend, and that the only reason he accepted the invitation was because he just couldn't tell his friend "no."

John's wife exploded! The children were disappointed. In frustration John stormed out of the house, harshly reminding his family that he deserved some time to do what he wanted to do. The day seemed long, though, to John. His golf game went from bad to horrible. As luck would have it, the course was playing very slowly that day. John was miserable.

As the sun went down, John drove into his driveway. The children were finishing their baths. As he walked into the house, John felt a chill in the air. Little did he know that his trouble was just beginning.

John had not handled the shuffle very well. He did not connect outwardly with those around him, especially with the people who were most important to him. What was his problem?

John's problem was that he had the wrong priorities. The decisions he made that day mirrored what was important to him. His wrong priorities resulted in his making some poor decisions. These poor decisions hurt John as well as everyone around him.

John's story is a common one in many families today. He failed in his outward connection to others because his priorities were not correct. This problem can be multiplied countless times in families everywhere because of the failure to have the right priorities.

A Guide for God's Priorities

Our priorities should be determined by the Word of God. Jesus shared an important guide for us to follow in establishing God's priorities. Jesus says in Matthew 6:33:

But seek first His kingdom and His righteousness; and all these things shall be added to you.

This verse provides an excellent guide for determining our priorities.

Jesus tells us that we need to pursue the kingdom of God with great intensity. What is the kingdom of God? In Romans 14:17 the Bible tells us that the kingdom of God is the following:

The kingdom of God is not eating and drinking, but righteousness and peace and joy in the Holy Spirit.

We are further reminded in 1 Corinthians 4:20 that:

The kingdom of God does not consist in word, but in power.

In other words, the kingdom of God is the experience of the power of God's Spirit. This experience results in righteousness, peace, and joy. It is the ultimate experience of the upward connection with God.

Jesus also challenges us to pursue His righteousness. The righteousness of God is His standard. His standard is excellence. It is holiness. The righteousness of God is being in right standing with Him because of a proper relationship with Him.

The result of this is that the things that we are tempted to worry about, such as eating, drinking, and clothing, will be given to us. As we focus on these temporal things, they become interruptions in our lives. Many times these interruptions lead us to disconnect from God, ourselves, and others. But God has promised that if we will pursue the ultimate connection with Him, we will discover in the Holy Spirit all the temporal things that we need. Therefore, we have no need to be stressed out about such things.

There are three principles that serve as God's guide to helping us establish our priorities. These principles are found in Matthew 6:33. The first is . . .

Do not be sidetracked with the temporal. David and Ann had been struggling in their relationship with God and one another. As they left church one Sunday, they asked me if they could arrange to have an appointment with me. I instructed them to call my office and schedule one the next day.

When they arrived they began to share their story. After listening to them talk for fifteen minutes, I could easily see the cause of their problem. They had been so caught up in obtaining certain possessions that they had fallen into financial bondage. This financial stress clouded everything in their personal lives as well as their marriage. I shared with them the importance of Matthew 6:33 and challenged them to permit this verse to serve as God's guide in setting their priorities. David and Ann had become sidetracked with temporal things.

We do not need to make the same mistake this young couple made. However, the only way that temporal things will not sidetrack us is if we establish the correct priorities. Jesus' words challenge us to not be distracted by temporal things.

The passage in Matthew 6 provides a second principle that should serve as our guide in determining priorities. This principle is . . .

Pursue only that which lasts forever. Years ago when I was a seminary student, I became deeply convicted that everything in my life needed to have an eternal element in it. I began to understand that as I gave of the resources God had entrusted to me, I was making an eternal investment. I then committed that I would grow in the area of giving every year. This commitment was the result of my desire to invest only in things that have eternal value.

When we are distracted by the temporal things of life, it is difficult to pursue things that last forever. We demonstrate through our decisions whether or not we are pursuing after that which lasts eternally. Whether it be in regard to our purchases, our career decisions, or our goals, we are to pursue after that which lasts forever. This principle is further explained by another truth that is found in Matthew 6:33, which is . . .

A right relationship with God is all that lasts forever. It is a sobering thought for me to understand that out of all the things I have to do or choose to do, the only thing that lasts forever is a right relationship to God. I can help people, pray for them, minister to them, counsel with them, and love them, but the only thing that lasts forever is for all of us to have a right relationship with our Creator. I can travel the world preaching the gospel, building churches, and feeding people, but the only thing that lasts forever is for everyone I help, including myself, to have a right relationship to Him.

This is why we need to have the personal relationship to God that is available only through Jesus Christ. This is why we need to spend daily time with God in His Word. This is why we need to learn to communicate with Him through prayer. This is why we need to journalize our spiritual walk with Christ. This is why we need to place our entire life and resources in sharing the gospel with people throughout the world. A right relationship to God is all that lasts forever!

The only way we can follow God's guiding principles that are taught in Matthew 6:33 is by establishing the right priorities. We will not be sidetracked with temporal things when our priorities are right. We will pursue only that which lasts forever when our priorities are right. Our relationship to Christ will be right only when we have the proper priorities. Therefore, we will only be able to relate well to others in the outward connection when we have the right priorities.

It is significant that we understand . . .

God's Game Plan for Our Lives

When the Dallas Cowboys defeated the Buffalo Bills in the 1993 Super Bowl game in Pasadena, California, it was obvious that they successfully completed their game plan. The coaches spent hours developing the strategy that was needed to defeat Buffalo. They taught the game plan to their players. Then they worked with them on the field. On game day, the Cowboys were prepared. They were ready to defeat their opponent because they knew what their game plan was and they followed it. The final score was Dallas 52, Buffalo 17. The Cowboys' game plan reflected their priorities and earned them the world championship title.

Just as this outstanding team had a game plan for the Buffalo Bills, God has a game plan for how we are to live. Every game plan reflects what is considered to be important. Therefore, our game plan for life will reflect our priorities. God's game plan reflects His priorities for our lives.

There are five areas that sooner or later will be prioritized in our lives. The key to having integrity is to have these areas in line with God's priorities. Our goal should be to please God by our lives reflecting what we say we believe. We have accountability because our lives never lie to us.

What should our priorities be?

Priority #1

Personal relationship and fellowship with God. From the time I made a commitment to give the first hour of every day to God, I have never been sorry. My relationship to Jesus Christ is my first priority. Having the honor of fellowship with God is why I spend the first hour of my day with Him. As I have already shared, this time with the Father involves reading His Word, praying, and writing in a spiritual journal. I do not read the newspaper until I have spent this time with God. In fact, I do not do anything or see anyone until I have met with my Heavenly Father. My relationship and fellowship with Him is of the ultimate importance in my life.

Our priorities need to begin with our relationship to God. Everything else must be secondary. This development of our upward connection with God has the potential to set all other things in order. If we want to live orderly, balanced, and spiritually powerful lives, then we must begin our day by developing our relationship to Him through fellowship with Jesus Christ, His Son.

Is this the first priority of your life? How important is your personal devotional life? If you do anything daily before you spend time with God, then your relationship and fellowship with God is not your number one priority. When your relationship and fellowship with Him is your first priority, your life will at least have the potential to be orderly. Balance comes only when we have fellowship with God. Spiritual power does not come through a flesh-filled life, but through a Spirit-controlled life. The only way to be Spirit-controlled is by spending time with God and experiencing fellowship with Him. This experience will result in spiritual power and in being rightly related or outwardly connected to the temporal things around us. This is the first step to having spiritual success. When a person spends this time with God at the beginning of every day, then he is ready for the next priority of life.

Priority #2

Family. Following my relationship to God and fellowship with Him, I can honestly say that my family is my second priority. My goal every Friday is to spend quality time with my wife. On Saturday my goal is to spend quality time with my two boys. During the week I attempt to arrange my schedule to meet my family's pressing needs. Unless it is absolutely impossible, such as if I have to be out of the city, I attend every ball game, every musical, and every other event in which Josh and Nicholas participate. In fact, at times I turn down engagements or rearrange my schedule when I am away in order to come back early so I can be a part of these events. I want my family to know that after Jesus and before anything else, they are my priority. Lip service means nothing, but my presence means everything to them.

When we are committed to our families, we are setting ourselves up for success in family life instead of failure. We must do the little things as well as the big things in order to convey to our families how much we love them. We must sacrifice for one another for the family team to be successful. Fragmented families are the result of bad priorities. Families that are together, relating well to one another, for the most part are families who have God as their first priority and each other as their second priority. Therefore, if we desire to save our families, we must have them in the right order of our priorities.

Is your family important to you? Remember, your life never lies. If you are married, consider your relationship with your spouse and answer the following questions.

- Do you love your spouse with a sacrificial love?
- Are you willing to suffer for him or her?
- Are you praying for your spouse's needs?
- Do you even know your spouse's needs?
- Are you communicating with your spouse?
- Are you honoring your spouse?

- Are you faithful to your spouse physically as well as mentally?
- Do you ever surprise your spouse with something special?
- Are you still courting your spouse?
- Do you give gifts on his or her birthday?
- Do you give your spouse a special gift at Christmas?

Do not forget. Your life tells you how important your relationship is to your spouse. How did you do in answering those questions?

Let me challenge you to look at your relationship to your children and grandchildren through the following questions.

- Are you critical of your children?
- Are you irritable with them?
- Are you overly strict with your children?
- Is your discipline inconsistent with them?
- Are you favoring one child over another?
- Are you tender verbally and physically with them?
- Do you love them enough to discipline them?
- Do you teach your children spiritual principles?
- Do you attend their birthday parties?
- Are you present at their ball games?

The way you answer these questions testifies of your commitment to your family. Remember, do not appraise your commitment through your words; appraise it with your life. Your life never lies to you.

Once your relationship to God and fellowship with Him is determined as your first priority, you are on your way to reconnecting with God. When you have placed your family second in your list of what you consider important, you are ready to outwardly and properly connect with others.

What should be your next priority?

Priority #3

Church. I am convinced that I cannot live the Christian life apart from the local church. My parents taught me this when I was a child. My parents always made decisions that reflected the importance of the church. Now that I am a pastor, it is difficult for me to be objective about this priority. However, my church is where I learn many lessons that help me grow spiritually. It is in the church that I receive the support and love that I need to get me through the difficult times in life. The church serves as my spiritual foundation. I am thankful for it. My fellow believers provide me with fellowship, accountability, and encouragement when I need it.

The church is not a building. It is a group of people who believe in Jesus Christ as Lord and Savior, as well as the major fundamentals of the Christian faith. My church building could burn down today, but the church would shine brighter than ever tomorrow.

Jesus died for the church. We are the church. Christ is our Head. Therefore, I can never be committed to Jesus Christ and not be committed to His church. There is a movement in some Christian ranks that places the church in a low priority. This is demonstrated in many ways.

We must let the church be the center of our lives. It should be the place where we find fellowship, acceptance, love, and purpose. We must never buy into a "here today and gone tomorrow" mentality. Many people have the attitude, "If the church does not meet my needs, then I'll leave and find one that does." Churches are like individuals. They go through various seasons in life— times of struggle and times of prosperity. Disloyalty to the church demonstrates a disloyalty to Jesus Christ.

Will you honestly face where you are with your church? Will you let it be the most important fellowship in your life, following your commitment to Christ and to your family? I urge you to consider the following questions.

- Do you attend your church's weekly worship services?
- Are you growing spiritually through your local church?
- Are you serving the church by using the spiritual gifts God has given to you?
- Are you participating in your church's efforts to take the gospel to the entire world?
- Are you giving at least one-tenth of your income to your church?
- Are you inviting your friends and family members to attend worship with you?
- Are you supporting your senior pastor with love, encouragement, and prayer?

- Are you encouraging those who serve with him by helping them to accomplish their God-given ministry assignments?
- Are you only speaking well of your church?

Your life does not lie to you, so where are you in your relationship to your church? Your priorities should then be to have God as your first priority, your family as your second priority, followed by your church as your third priority. What should be your next priority?

Priority #4

Job. Keeping our desires and goals for a career in perspective under God's priority is probably one of the greatest challenges we face. I believe this is especially a common struggle among men. We are under the eyes of those around us and often feel the pressure to be successful in our profession. This pressure is felt by those in the ministry as much as in any profession. It comes from my peers as well as from the people whom I have been called to pastor. It comes from a world system whose mentality has invaded the church in America.

We need to remember that our jobs are important, but they are not more important than our families. It is a challenge to keep our jobs in the proper order of priorities. We all have a tendency to neglect spending time with God because of the demands of our work. But we must never allow this to happen. Our careers have a tendency to jeopardize our relationship with our families, but we must also refuse to let this happen. The pressures from our job often creeps into our lives and convinces us that we do not have time to attend or serve our local church. We must never buy these lies of Satan! God wants us to do well on our job, but never at the expense of Him, our family, or our church.

Christians should be the best employees in the workplace.

- Are you enthusiastic about your job?
- Do you give your job your whole heart?
- Is excellence your standard in every task you are assigned?
- Are you willing to pay the price to make your company or corporation successful?

- Are you honoring God by having the highest integrity possible while you are on the job? Are you in submission to your supervisor?
- Are you playing like a team player or are you insisting on "doing your own thing?" Take the high road in your job. Do your work as unto the Lord.

The last priority in God's game plan for our lives is . . .

Priority #5

Recreation. I am very fortunate to live in a place that is far removed from the recreation that I enjoy the most. Therefore, the temptation is not as great for me to spend more time than I should enjoying this favorite pastime. I love to snow ski. For the past few years I have been able to go twice a year. If my schedule and budget would permit, I would love to go more often. It is when I am on the slopes that I am able to forget all the other cares of life. At that time everything back at my office becomes somewhat insignificant to me. In fact, I do not even think about the office. I love the mountains, the cold, the snow, and the entire experience of snow skiing.

We are a generation that plays. We love to play all kinds of games and participate in all kinds of sports. There is nothing wrong with recreation, but it is extremely important to keep it in the right order of God's game plan for our lives. For some reason, recreation has a tendency to get our lives out of balance. Beware of this tendency and make sure that God is honored even in your recreation.

- Is your play or recreation in the right order?
- Do you work as hard at being a good father as you do at being a good golfer?
- Do you get more thrill from attending a ball game than you do from being in the presence of God?
- Is your physical fitness more important than your relationship to your spouse?
- Does your recreation ever prevent you from attending church?

- Does your recreation cloud your commitment to your job and thereby rob your employer of your focus and best efforts?
- Are you a better fan than you are a better Christian?

There is nothing wrong with recreation. I believe God wants us to be involved in recreation, but never at His expense, our family's expense, our church's expense, or our job's expense. In our day of play, one of our greatest challenges is to maintain a balance in this area.

Our outward connection with people and things is only in order when we are upwardly connected with God and inwardly aware of who we are in Christ. If we are to model order, balance, and spiritual power, we will do so only when we have the right priorities. We need to follow God's guiding principles that we find in Matthew 6:33 as our game plan for life.

Was the Buffalo Bills' game plan less effective than the Dallas Cowboys' game plan in the 1993 Super Bowl game? Obviously the Bills' game plan was inferior to the Cowboys' strategy. But the Bills also had a major problem executing their game plan. In fact, their game plan might have been successful if certain interruptions to it had not occurred. Once those began, the Bills became disconnected with their game plan. As a result, they failed miserably in this particular game.

We can have our own game plan for our lives, or we can follow the game plan that God has designed for us. However, our own plan will definitely be inferior to God's plan. We will have a difficult time executing our plan because the priorities will be wrong. We will face numerous interruptions from a fast paced society to a major crisis. Interruptions are a part of life. However, when these interruptions come, we tend to disconnect from God. The result is spiritual failure.

The key to successful decision-making is to have the right game plan for our lives and then to execute that plan. Sometimes we view decision-making as a difficult task. However, it is relatively simple when God's game plan is used. When we have to make a decision about any area of life, we can simply consider our priorities and allow them to make our decision for us. This is how we execute God's game plan for our lives. This is also what prevents the interruptions of life from distracting us from God's priorities for us.

Never play mind games with yourself. Do not try to rationalize the decisions you must make. You can lie to yourself mentally about what you consider to be your priorities. However, your life never lies. Examine your life and look at how you are relating to God and to others. This is the outward connection that leads to order, balance, and spiritual power.

Then take a look beyond priorities. Are you living in . . .

11

Confusion or Order?

ON JANUARY 1, 1979, I BE-
came the pastor of First Baptist Church of Milford, Texas. This was
my first full-time pastorate. Jeana and I were very excited about
moving to this small town of seven hundred people. We were
going to be able to live in the parsonage, which was located next
door to the church. Milford was only a little over an hour's drive
from Fort Worth, Texas, where Southwestern Baptist Theological
Seminary is located. I received both of my theological degrees
from the seminary.

Milford was a quiet town. Most of the people who lived there
were nice, simple people. A sign outside the town read:

Milford: The Home of 700 Friendly People
and Three or Four Old Grouches.

I have to admit that there were times when I felt that those three
or four grouches were all members of my congregation. During
the three years that I served as pastor of this church, my wife and
I were blessed and the power of the Holy Spirit was evident in our
ministry.

One of my greatest challenges during these years was to have
a life of order rather than confusion. Our church was growing. I
was serving as a full-time pastor in addition to taking fourteen to

sixteen hours each semester at seminary. Every Tuesday through Friday I would get up early and have my devotional time with God. Then I traveled fifteen miles to join other preachers to car pool to seminary. We would arrive at the campus in time for our 8 a.m. class. Our school day would conclude by 2 p.m., and I would arrive back in Milford by 3:30 p.m. Then I attempted to tend to the ministry needs of the church. For three years every day of my life was filled with responsibilities from early in the morning until late in the evening.

When Joshua was born in 1980, the challenge to maintain order intensified. I was just beginning work on my doctorate degree and was feebly trying to help my wife with our first child. On many days I felt my life and ministry were in total confusion. There was no time for me personally. When I look back on those three years of ministry, family life, and schooling, I realize that it was only by the grace of God that I survived.

I believe that the only reason God's grace was able to bring me through these difficult days was because of my personal devotion to Christ and my commitment to the right priorities in life. I understood that my seminary education was only for a season rather than for a lifetime. I was so grateful to have the opportunity to minister full-time to a church while I faced the challenge of academic education. This pastorate helped me to balance the classroom learning with the on-the-job training for being a pastor. It was difficult for me to endure, but without a doubt, this time was probably more difficult for my wife. She had to sacrifice far more than I did.

When I experienced a feeling of confusion, my goal became merely to survive. When I felt a time of order, I then felt fulfilled in every area of my life. I was able to experience order much more than confusion. Perhaps the greatest lesson I learned from this experience was discipline. I learned to set priorities, plan, use time effectively, and get things done quickly. Personal discipline was essential in bringing order to my schedule. The lesson of personal discipline I learned in these three years has been one of the greatest assets of my ministry, family, and personal success that God has granted me.

In the late 1980s there was a great deal of emphasis on getting ready for the 1990s. For the first time I could remember, many people seemed to express fear about how we would deal with the challenges of the next decade. As 1990 arrived it seemed that this was the year of testing all the preparation that people had made for this crucial time in history. However, by the time 1991 arrived, we had stopped living in fear of the 1990s. All conversation and attention began to focus on the 21st century. This race toward the next century adds to the stress people are already experiencing. We are living in the 21st century as though it has arrived. However, we must not let this attitude rob the joy of today.

When we do not understand who we are in relationship to who God is, we experience an identity problem. When our desires are not to honor God and give Him glory, we live unfulfilled lives. When we do not follow God's game plan for our lives by having the right priorities and by executing our decision-making by using these priorities, we become a victim . . . of the rat race!

What We Lose as Victims of the Rat Race

Alan could not understand why he felt so much pressure. His feeling of stress was at an all-time high. He had experienced a great deal of success at his corporation. Alan was a young man rapidly making his way up the career ladder. Even though he was single, the demands on Alan's life were increasing. Personal time was almost non-existent. The only thing Alan did was work six days a week, come to church on Sunday, and eat on the run daily. When Alan was finally able to go home from work, it was always late and he was very tired. Alan shared with me that he felt he was in a race and could never catch up.

I began to quiz Alan about his personal walk with Christ. I asked him to share with me about the personal time he spent with the Lord. Alan explained that he used to have a quiet time with God every morning. However, because his schedule was now so demanding and his rest was so limited, Alan just did not get up early like he used to in order to have his time with God. This young man was a victim of the rat race and had lost his daily fellowship with God. As a result, Alan felt stressed, frustrated, and confused as to why he no longer had any control over his schedule.

Fellowship with God

When we become victims of the rat race, we lose one spiritual experience. This experience is the most important of all. It is our fellowship with God.

Is the same thing that happened to Alan happening to you? If you are feeling frustration, pressure, and stress, is it because you are neglecting your time with God? The result of this negligence will be that you will strain your fellowship with Him.

While Moses was on the mountain of God receiving the commandments for the people of Israel, Aaron was acting as the spiritual leader of God's people. The people began to place great pressure upon Aaron. He must have felt that he was trapped in what we call the "rat race" of life. Aaron became distracted by this pressure and began to limit his time of fellowship with his Heavenly Father. As a result, the people of God suffered. As they became disconnected from God, these people proceeded to make a golden calf and turned their devotion to it. This resulted in God's judgment upon them.

When we are victims of the rat race, rather than victors in the rat race, we lose our fellowship with God. Please note that I am not saying we lose our relationship to God, but we do lose our fellowship with Him. We lose that day-by-day experience of walking with Jesus. We lose the privilege of being in continual communion with Him.

A practical thing that we lose as we become victims of the rat race is . . .

Order

In the story above I shared how Alan lost order in his life as he became a victim of his schedule. Spiritually, he lost his fellowship with God. Practically, Alan's life lost its order. He came to realize that he had no control over any area of his life. His circumstances led him to crisis manage his life rather than manage it under God's control. This type of lifestyle always results in a lack of order.

When Samson was in fellowship with God, he lived an orderly life. As he lost this fellowship by disobeying God's will, he started downward in his spiritual life. As the result of compromising his principles, he lost his power. This is when he also lost order in his life. Samson was then taken into captivity by the Philistines and became their target of abuse. Everything began to come apart in Samson's life.

When we are victims of the rat race, we lose order in our lives. Our schedules seem to become more demanding, as well as the expectations of others. Our focus then becomes blurred when we lose order. It seems that we lose control of everything around us. Things begin to run us rather than our running them.

As victims of the rat race, we not only lose order, but we also lose . . .

Balance

As I listened to Alan relate what had happened to him, I sensed that he had little balance in his life. Because of his demanding schedule, Alan simply submitted to that extremity rather than trying to bring about some balance to his work life, personal life, and spiritual life. The rat race had tilted Alan's life so that it focused only on one of these areas rather than having a balance. Balance became foreign to him. Alan reached the point where he felt it was impossible to achieve balance any longer.

Earlier in this book I recalled the struggles of King David as a follower of God. When David began to drift away from fellowship with his heavenly Father, his whole life lost its balance. Perhaps the role of leadership finally caught up with him. Maybe he was so stressed from his leadership responsibilities that he neglected going to battle as the king. One moment David was a man after God's own heart, and the next moment he was attempting to cover up his sin. He went from one extreme to the other. What happened to him? His disconnectedness from God and the pressures of his life resulted in his becoming a victim of the rat race. As a consequence, David lost the balance in his life.

Maintaining balance is a tremendous challenge. We are all tempted to live by simply responding to the desires of those who yell the loudest for our attention. Whether it be our jobs, our families, our church, or some other pressures in life, we are challenged to live a life that is focused by refusing to let it get out of balance. To accomplish this balance requires that we have discernment. It also requires that we be disciplined.

The real tragedy of being a victim of the rat race, rather than a victor in it, is that we permit things to rule over us. God's will is for us to do the ruling, to have dominion of, or to be faithful stewards of our lives. This is impossible if we are victims of the rat race.

We were created to have fellowship with God. Our purpose is to honor Him. We are here to bring glory to Him in all that we do. We were created to worship God! We are here to show His worth to Him and to others. In order to escape confusion and experience order, we need to be aware of some . . .

Principles of Worship That Transcend Our Lives

As a pastor, I am a worship leader. My role every Sunday is to lead God's people to encounter Him. If I fail in accomplishing this goal, then I feel that we have missed experiencing God. Yet, I am totally aware that my role as a public worship leader will never be more effective than my own experience of worship every day. This is also true of every believer who participates in the Sunday worship experience. Every person has to be involved in daily worship of God in order for public worship to be a dynamic experience.

Since we were created to fellowship with God and worship Him, then surely the same principles that are true in our public worship will also be true of our private worship experience. These principles should transcend our personal lives. We worship Christ personally by walking with Him in every area of our lives. The first of these principles of worship that should transcend our personal lives is . . .

God Is Not a God of Confusion

When the apostle Paul instructed the church on the subject of worship, he was instructing us about a principle in life that we should always remember. This principle is that God is not a God of confusion. The Bible states in 1 Corinthians 14:33:

For God is not a God of confusion but of peace, as in all the churches of the saints.

In public worship there should not be confusion; there should always be peace. By peace I do not mean passivity but clarity as to what God is saying and doing among His people.

148

When we are victors in the rat race, rather than victims of it, it is because we are not living in confusion. Many times we are at the mercy of our schedules and the expectations of others. The result is confusion. When we attempt to live our lives based on the opinions of others or based on our own performance for a sense of worth, then we will live in confusion.

We must understand that if we are living in confusion, then we are living out of the will of God. If our lives are continually turned upside down and inside out, then we are experiencing confusion. This confusion is not God's will for our lives. He wants us to experience fellowship with Him, peace in the affairs of life, and balance in our lives. The mark of being a victim of the rat race is confusion.

Another principle of worship that should transcend our lives is . . .

Let All Things Be Done in Order

In 1 Corinthians 14 the apostle Paul continues his instructions concerning worship. Another principle of worship that should transcend our lives is to let all things be done in order. 1 Corinthians 14:40 states:

But let all things be done properly and in an orderly manner.

Just as God wants things done properly and orderly in public worship, He desires these same characteristics to mark our personal lives.

When we are in fellowship with God and have an order and balance to our lives, then we are acting as victors in the rat race of life. Whether it be in our schedules, our circumstances, or our relationship to people or things, there should be order. This is a mark of godly behavior, indicating that we have a proper relationship to God.

As I have ministered to people in various churches across our country, I have realized that there is a tremendous lack of order in the lives of many people. Order almost seems to be a thing of the past. But this is not God's will. He wants our lifestyles to present order.

It is not only in men's lives that the "shuffle" I referred to earlier is present. It is more apparent in lives of women than ever before. The shuffle is often seen in the lives of our children. We all have so many options to consider. These options have ceased to be a convenience to us; they have often become opportunities for bondage. God wants us to have order in the shuffle rather than confusion. The only way this will happen is when we know who we are in the Lord, determine to glorify God in all things, and live by the priorities that God has ordered for our lives. Once again, personal discipline is absolutely necessary for us to allow God's will to be done through us. These principles of worship should transcend our lives in every area. God's will is for an orderly life, not a confused life.

Now that we have looked at what God's Word says about order and confusion, let us consider some . . .

Practical Suggestions to Bring Order to Our Lives

When I communicate with people Sunday by Sunday, they appreciate biblical exposition. However, they always want it to be accompanied with relevance and practicality in its application. Otherwise, they feel that their time has been wasted.

I know that this mindset is present all across America. People must have their "felt" needs met before they can see the real need in their lives. Therefore, since we know it is not God's will for us to experience confusion, let us consider some practical suggestions that will help bring order to our lives. The first suggestion is . . .

Put Everything We Must Do on a Calendar

I am amazed at how many people live their lives by "shooting from the hip." Many move from crisis to crisis, never really having a hold on their lives. They miss appointments, forget obligations, and unintentionally neglect responsibilities, all because of their failure to take steps that will bring order to their lives.

For years I have lived by a calendar. I now live by a high-tech calendar called "Wizard." All my appointments, obligations, and responsibilities can be entered into this device. As a result I have an order to my schedule. My wife also lives by a calendar by writing down all the responsibilities of our family. This helps to bring order to all our lives.

We must learn to put everything we must do on a calendar. It does not have to be a fancy calendar or a high-tech device. Each day we should make a list of things that must be done. There is a good feeling of joy and a sense of motivation that is derived when a person is able to check off each item on the list. It helps a person even more if he follows his priorities as he accomplishes his daily tasks.

Another practical suggestion is...

Write "Taken" on All Birthdays and Anniversaries

The birthdays of my immediate family are very important to me. Everything I do on these birth dates as well as on my wedding anniversary is secondary to my responsibilities as a father or as a husband. Therefore, I mark these dates on my calendar as taken.

I am surprised at how many fathers miss their children's birthday parties. I am amazed at how many people forget the birthdays of their loved ones. I do not understand a mindset that dismisses anniversaries as insignificant. If a person is unable to remember these dates, he must consider them to be unimportant.

Therefore, a person should mark all special dates as "taken" on his calendar. All of our children's special events should become a part of calendar planning. The only way our lives will ever be organized and personally sensitive to the ones we love most is by bringing order to it. Planning our schedules is essential if we are going to reach the goal of bringing order to our lives.

Another practical suggestion is . . .

Schedule Vacations

There is nothing worse than going through a year without some days being set aside for refreshment and vacation. When this is neglected, we become exhausted and ineffective. God wants us to take time away from the busy pace of our lives in order to rest. An annual vacation can supply this time of relaxation.

Regardless of our financial status, we can do something for a family vacation. This time may simply involve a weekend away where lodging and dining are inexpensive. Families need to have the experience of bonding that can come only through this special time.

I attempt to take two to three weeks of vacation with my family every year. We spend one of these weeks traveling to see our parents. I spend another of these weeks with just my wife and children. We also find time to spend other days together throughout the year.

When it is possible, Jeana and I periodically try to get away together. This may be once a quarter or once every six months. A night or two away from the children gives us an opportunity to renew our relationship. Almost any couple can accomplish such a time by simply planning it. There are wonderful hotel chains that provide great weekend rates. Taking advantage of these opportunities will be very beneficial to a person's marriage.

Another practical suggestion is . . .

Only Commit to What You Really Need to or Want to Do

For years I thought that I needed to be at the beck and call of all the members of my church. I also felt that I could not miss any meeting that my denomination asked me to attend. Anytime someone asked me to do anything, I felt I had a responsibility to do it.

In recent years I have learned to commit to do only the things I really need to do or want to do. I have learned that I do not have to meet everyone's needs. I am not God. I have learned that I do not have to be at every meeting that is scheduled. These meetings go on whether or not I am present. I have also learned that ministry to the members of my church can also be accomplished by other pastors on my staff or by some of our laypersons. I do not have to be involved in everything in order for our church to be effective and successful.

Every person should learn these lessons that I have finally learned. We should commit to do only those things that we really need to do or really want to do. You are not God either. Do not try to be Him. Things can go on without your being present. Our priorities should determine what we need to do rather than the requests or the expectations of others.

We need to accompany the above with one final practical suggestion, which is . . .

Learn to Say No!

I have learned to say no to others. I have survived by saying no to them. I do not like to tell people no. I do not delight in it. However, if I am going to be a man of great devotion to God, a great husband and father, and a great pastor, I cannot do everything people expect me to do or want me to do. Therefore, I have learned to say no!

My priorities in life and the priorities in my ministry determine what I do. These priorities determine what I say "yes" to and what I say "no" to at any time.

Let me encourage you to learn to say no. At times this is the proper thing to do. In fact, sometimes the most spiritual thing a person can do is to say no. This is the way our priorities will win in our lives. When our priorities are God's priorities and we live by them, then we will experience order, balance, and spiritual power.

Are you living in confusion or order? Which one of these words characterize your life? If it is confusion, then you are not experiencing the outward connection, which results in your being rightly related to the people and affairs in your life. If your life is characterized by order, then you are experiencing the outward connection, which results in your being rightly related to the people and affairs in your life. God has not made you to live a life of confusion but of order. When you live by God's priorities and are willing to execute them in every area of your life,then the result will be that you will experience order, balance, and spiritual power.

We are now prepared to move to the climactic experience of culminating this outward connection. This will come only as we are. . .

Preparing to face life's real issues.

12

Preparing to Face Life's Real Issues

THROUGHOUT OUR LIVES we are continually bombarded with a myriad of challenges. From the time I was a child until now, I have constantly faced critical challenges. I have come to realize that many challenges that seemed great at the time were really tools God was using to prepare me for what was ahead. I now believe that every challenge we face is a preparation for our final challenge, which is death.

The biggest challenge I faced as a child was learning to deal with an older brother and sister. I had a difficult time understanding why they received so many privileges that I was denied because I was "the baby of the family." My biggest challenge as a teenager was learning to live for Jesus Christ in the midst of pressure from my peers to live like the world. As a college student my greatest challenge was to keep my heart on fire for God in the middle of a highly academic environment. During my seminary days, I quickly realized that my biggest challenge would be to maintain balance and order while being a student, pastor, husband, and father. Once my seminary work was completed, I learned that as a pastor my greatest challenge was to lead God's people into greatness in the most effective manner possible and to help them fulfill God's vision for them as a church. As a father my greatest challenge is to do all that I can to see that my sons grow up in love with Jesus and committed to His cause in the world.

God used each of these challenges from my past to prepare me for one of the greatest challenges of my life, which was to walk through a major crisis with my wife as she battled with cancer.

It was very difficult for me to watch someone I loved so much have to deal with this threatening illness in such a young season of her life. It was difficult to see my wife undergo major surgery and then be unable to function at full capacity for months. It was challenging to see this young, vibrant woman endure months of radiation and chemotherapy treatments that ultimately caused the total loss of her beautiful hair and at times the loss of her strength. It was difficult to watch my wife struggle emotionally at times, until God would step in and deliver her. It was a challenge to be as selfless as I needed to be so God could use me to meet my wife's needs. However, it is now a joy to know that Jeana is healed. Praise be to God!

I believe that everyone of these challenges have been God's preparing me to deal with my current challenges as well as future challenges of which I am not even aware at this time. If Jesus does not come before I die, I fully believe that every challenge I will have faced in my lifetime is for the purpose of preparing me for the ultimate challenge of all, the challenge of death.

Every believer needs to understand how God's process of working in our lives is for the purpose of preparing us for the real issues we must face. Years ago I heard the following statement, which I have never forgotten: "The process always precedes the product."

We always want the outcome of all we do (the product) to be successful. However, the product is always the result of the process. If we do not like the product, then we must change the process.

For example, if we are not properly responding outwardly to the persons and things we face, then we must change our process of preparation. This outward connection is totally dependent on whether or not we are upwardly connected with God. As this upward connection is experienced, then we become inwardly aware of who we really are in Christ. It is then, and only then, that we are ready to face the outward connection of people, things, and the challenges we must face.

We have seen this process expressed by looking at the life of Isaiah the prophet. We know that he first experienced the upward connection with God when he saw the Lord. When Isaiah experienced this, he then came to realize who he was. Once he realized this inward connection, he saw himself as sinful and broken, but forgiven. After he went through this process, Isaiah was ready for the outward connection.

This outward connection in Isaiah's life had to do with God's call to him. God's call and Isaiah's response is recorded in Isaiah 6:8, which says:

Then I heard the voice of the Lord, saying, "Whom shall I send, and who will go for Us?" Then I said, "Here am I, Send me!"

Isaiah was aware that the messenger whom God was going to call was not going to receive a great response from the people. He knew that the words would fall upon hardened hearts that were not ready to respond to God's message to them.

However, Isaiah had seen the Lord. He had seen the hosts of heaven ministering to him. The majesty of God and His holiness were more real to Isaiah than ever before. Then he heard the voice of God. It came in the form of this question, "Whom shall I send and who will go for us?" After Isaiah had seen and heard God, he quickly and willingly responded, "Here am I, send me." Isaiah felt he had no choice but to go, once he had experienced God as he had. So Isaiah told the Lord that he would go and share His message with the people.

As a result of this process, Isaiah had first looked upward, then inward, and then outward. He connected upwardly and inwardly, then was ready to connect outwardly. This is also the process God uses to prepare us to face the real issues of life. This is what real worship is all about. Real worship involves corporate worship in our churches as well as private worship which we do personally. As we experience God and come to realize who we are in the Lord, then we are ready to deal with the real issues of life.

Once Isaiah had seen the Lord and realized his own condition, he made himself totally available to God. He was willing to be God's servant by allowing the Lord to use him in any way.

When we are upwardly and inwardly connected in the right manner, we will also be totally available to God. Our attitude needs to be, "Lord, whatever you ask of me, my answer is yes." This is real availability. Real availability is unconditional, regardless of the request.

Once Isaiah upwardly connected with God and inwardly with himself, he was willing to do whatever God wanted him to do. He was willing to live the rest of his life, knowing that God's message would be rejected as he shared it with others. But Isaiah was willing to preach to hard hearts and walk through life as a lonely prophet of God.

Just as Isaiah was willing to do whatever God asked of him, we will be willing to do whatever God wants us to do once we have upwardly connected with Him and inwardly connected with ourselves. A willing life is a great testimony to one's walk with God. We must be willing to go anywhere and do anything God asks us to do. A rational response to God's call is unacceptable. Once we become followers of Christ, we no longer belong to ourselves; we belong to Him. Therefore, we are to be available to Him and willing to do whatever He wants us to do.

We become prepared to face the real issues of life only after we have connected with God and experienced the fullness of that connection. After we have done this, we are then able to connect inwardly with who we really are in relationship to who God is. This is God's preparation for getting us ready to face the issues of life, or what could be referred to as the outward connection. Every issue we face is an issue of the heart.

When Jesus was teaching his followers how to relate to these outward issues in life, such as persons, possessions, and possibilities, He shared some powerful words. These words are recorded in Matthew 6:21:

For where your treasure is, there will your heart be also.

Jesus was teaching us that what we value will be seen in how we relate outwardly to persons, possessions, and possibilities. If we are relating to these in a spiritual way, honoring God in and through them, then it is evident that we have connected upwardly with God and inwardly with ourselves. The way we relate to these challenges will determine what we value. Therefore, these are issues of the heart.

One of the ways we need to prepare ourselves for facing these issues is by first understanding what these issues are. Since we now understand how God has used every challenge we have ever faced to prepare us for these issues, let me share about the twelve issues every person faces.

These twelve issues are ones that we all face daily. Each of them demands a godly response. The way we respond declares where we are with God and ourselves. When we respond properly to these issues, then we will live orderly, balanced, and powerful spiritual lives.

The first issue is . . .

Surrender

The apostle Paul always challenged the followers of Jesus to a surrendered life. One of his well-known challenges is found in Romans 12:1-2. In these verses Paul was inspired by the Holy Spirit to write:

I urge you therefore, brethren, by the mercies of God, to present your bodies a living and holy sacrifice, acceptable to God, which is your spiritual service of worship. And do not be conformed to this world, but be transformed by the renewing of your mind, that you may prove what the will of God is, that which is good and acceptable and perfect.

The challenge in this passage is for us to surrender our lives to God. Paul tells us that our daily surrendering to God is our spiritual service of worship. Through the continual surrendering of our lives to Him, we prove through our lives the will of God. It is God's will that we surrender continually to Him.

Every morning when we awake, the most important issue we must face is the issue of surrender. Are we willing to surrender our lives to God? This is a critical question each of us must answer. We must be willing to release every area of our lives to Him. As we do this, we will experience an upward connection with God. This will result in our dealing properly with ourselves as well as with the persons, possessions, and possibilities we face daily.

Let me challenge you to surrender your life to God every day. This is where we derive spiritual power. We must refuse to surrender to our own fleshly desires in order to give every area of our lives over to God.

The next issue we must face is . . .

Priorities

The setting of our priorities is one of the most critical issues with which we must deal. As we set our priorities, we must be certain that they are in alignment with God's Word. His priorities must become our priorities. We need to pursue God's kingdom in our priorities. In fact, His kingdom is our priority.

In chapter 10 of this book I outlined the following as God's priorities for our lives:

Priority #1 - Personal Relationship and Fellowship with God
Priority #2 - Family
Priority #3 - Church
Priority #4 - Job
Priority #5 - Recreation

It is critical that we set these God-given priorities as our game plan for life and then execute them in every decision we must make.

What are our priorities? Are they God's priorities? What is most important to us? Our priorities are an issue of our hearts. The things that are important to us are manifested in the priorities that we set. Every decision we make is an issue of priority. Therefore, every person must settle the issue of what his priorities will be in order for his life to be successful both spiritually and practically.

Another issue we face is . . .

Devotion

Our personal devotion to God is a critical issue. Our devotion to God is experienced through our personal time with God. As we spend time with Him, we should read His Word, communicate with Him through prayer, and document our walk with Him through the use of a spiritual journal. This time of devotion should be the first thing we do each day.

How is your devotional life? Is it consistent? Are you using it to let God speak to you through His Word? Are you communicating with Him through prayer? Are you journalizing your walk with Christ? Is your devotional life meaningful?

A day that begins in devotion with God is a day that can be lived in devotion to Him. Begin your day with God. Once you do this, anything else will be less than satisfactory to you.

Another issue we face is . . .

Time

One of the greatest gifts we enjoy is time. We should never take time for granted. It is precious and it is limited. Therefore, how we use our time is critical. The Bible says in Ephesians 5:16:

Making the most of your time, because the days are evil.

We are challenged to make the most of every opportunity. We are to redeem the time.

What are you doing with your time? Are you using it wisely? Could you be wasting precious time on insignificant things? Evaluate your use of time. Use it wisely. Use your time to glorify God.

The next important issue we face is . . .

Family

I have asked myself many times if I am willing to grow old, knowing that I have lost the loving affection of my wife and my children to the world because I placed other things before them. Since I began to ask myself this question, I have done my best to place my family high on my agenda. I never want to put anything before them, other than my personal relationship and fellowship with God.

Where does your family fit into your life? Are they important to you? Do they receive an important amount of your time? Do you adjust your schedule in order to meet their needs? You must never risk losing them as the result of placing other things before them. Possessions and position may be lost, but you will still have your family. Count them as special. Place them as a priority. Do not allow Satan to steal them from you.

We must also consider the issue of . . .

Finances

Our checkbook reflects our priorities. It reveals the spiritual condition of our heart. God has given us some great counsel regarding our finances in Malachi 3:10:

"Bring the whole tithe into the storehouse, so that there may be food in My house, and test Me now in this," says the Lord of hosts, "if I will not open for you the windows of heaven, and pour out for you a blessing until there is no more need."

God wants us to honor Him with one-tenth of all He has entrusted to us. This is called the tithe. Our finances are the only tangible way God has given us to demonstrate our love for Him. Honoring God with the tithe is an issue of the heart.

We should give to God. We must grow beyond honoring God with only the first tenth of our income. We need to move into the joy that comes from honoring Him beyond the tithe. As we learn to give sacrificially to God, He will bless us bountifully.

Also, we must beware of personal debt. Never should we presume on God. Instead, we need to maintain a balance in the area of personal debt. When we become in bondage to debt, the result can be catastrophic to our financial livelihood.

Next, consider . . .

Career

More and more people are seeking counseling in regard to their job or their career. The workplace is causing more frustration and pressure upon families than ever before. The heavy emphasis being placed on job performance has brought the issue of job or career to the forefront of the many issues we must face. As I counsel people in this area, I always try to bring the discussion back to the issue of priorities.

The most important issue we face in our relationship to our job or career is, "What importance should it have in my life?" We must also ask, "What place am I going to give it in my life?" These questions are at the heart of this issue.

As believers, God wants us to work hard. He wants us to have an outstanding work ethic. He also desires for us to be successful. At the same time, God wants us to keep our work in proper perspective. Our jobs should never run our lives. We must never permit our drive for a career to ruin our lives. This can happen if we do not keep it in perspective, but the only way to do this is by determining the priorities that are a part of God's game plan for our lives.

Another issue we must address is . . .

Church

Our spiritual life can never be all that God wants it to be until the church occupies an important place in our lives. What place should it occupy? Hebrews 10:25 reminds us:

Not forsaking our own assembling together, as is the habit of some, but encouraging one another; and all the more, as you see the day drawing near.

God places much importance on His people meeting together. He encourages us not to get caught up in the drift away from church that many believers are experiencing. Instead, He encourages us to be vitally involved in the ministries of the church.

As a pastor, I am convinced that a person cannot live the Christian life apart from the church. It is impossible to grow with God's people if we are not present with His people. The preaching and teaching of God's Word are imperative in the life of every Christian. We all need to experience worship weekly. As we encounter God through the corporate worship experience, we become motivated to live the Christian life.

Get involved in your church. Place yourself under the leadership of your pastor and staff and grow in the Lord. You will discover the real joy of the Christian life as you belong to, participate in, and grow with a local body of believers, which is the church.

The next issue we face is . . .

Mind

Everywhere we go our minds are being attacked by Satan. Billboards, television, radio, and other means of communication make it very difficult for believers to keep their minds on godly things. The real issue we must address is, "What are we going to think about?"

The Bible has a great deal to say about the mind. Philippians 4:8 says:

Finally, brethren, whatever is true, whatever is honorable, whatever is right, whatever is pure, whatever is lovely, whatever is of good repute, if there is any excellence and if anything worthy of praise, let your mind dwell on these things.

When we dwell on these things, we will not dwell on things that are ungodly. The key to controlling our thought life is what we allow to be taken into our minds. If we fill our minds with godliness, there will be no room for things that will distract us from God.

Next, we address . . .

Play

I believe recreation or play is very important. When we participate consistently in some area of recreation, our attitude towards the daily issues of life is improved. Recreation provides an important diversion that helps us maintain a better perspective on life. However, if play or recreation consumes our time and attention, it does not have the proper priority. This can be very detrimental to our Christian walk.

What place does recreation have in your life? Do you have a proper perspective toward it? Are you giving recreation more importance than it should receive? We must learn to have a healthy balance between play and work. When we do, we will be more effective in our Christian walk.

Next, consider the issue of . . .

Morality

I have never witnessed anything like the rampant immorality that exists in our country today. I believe this is happening because we have a generation of people that have been reared with the idea that there are no moral absolutes in life. Since our society has placed a decreasing emphasis on the Bible, humanists have been successful in propagating their agenda, which proclaims the total absence of moral absolutes.

The Bible is the Word of God. It is full of moral absolutes. Therefore, for morality to prevail, we must continually place God's Word in our minds. We must dismiss the mentality which says that moral absolutes are a thing of the past. Our challenge is to face this issue in both the private and the public areas of life. Morality is very important to the heart of God, so it should be important to us.

The final issue we will ever face is . . .

Death

Every challenge we face is a preparation for the final issue we all must face. This is the issue of death. Death is real. Just a few months ago I buried two young adults who were only 22 years old. Death is no respector of persons. It does not care what a person's age is. Death is an issue we will all confront.

Are you prepared to die? If you were diagnosed with a terminal illness today, would you be ready to die? If you were suddenly killed today, where would you spend eternity? The only way a person can be prepared to die is to have a personal relationship with Jesus Christ. By knowing Christ, we can face any type of challenge that death may present. Therefore, only as we know Jesus Christ personally will we effectively deal with the issue of death. There is no need to fear death when we know the Lord.

The only way to be successful in dealing with all the issues that have been mentioned is to reconnect daily with God. This is our only hope of living successfully in the outward connection.

God is always preparing us for the many challenges we must face. When we understand that this is a process of preparation, as it was with Isaiah, we will be ready to deal with the major issues we must address. Dealing with the issues of life is not merely survival; it is spiritual power that comes from God as the result of the dynamic relationship we are experiencing in our upward connection with Him.

We receive power in our Christian walk as we experience our upward connection with God. Our Christianity is deepened through our inward connection with ourselves as we discover who we are in relationship to who God is. However, our Christianity is demonstrated to others through our outward connection as we relate properly to other persons, our possessions, and all of the possibilities that God may bring our way. The key to each of these is the continual experience of reconnecting with God.

Conclusion

ALL BELIEVERS NEED TO experience unlimited communication with God. The distractions, interruptions, and pressures we face should never again lead us to drift away from Him. We must allow God to use these things to deepen our walk with Him, rather than allowing Satan to use them to disconnect us from God, possibly without even realizing it. God's will for our lives is not merely to survive these interruptions; He desires for us to have spiritual power over them and through them.

The only way a person can survive these distractions, interruptions, and pressures is to reconnect daily with God. Often we may find that we must continuously reconnect with Him. This is our power connection. This is the holy connection. This is the God connection. We must permit these obstacles to become God's opportunity to demonstrate His power through our lives.

When His power operates through us, God will bless our lives with order. We will not be thrown into chaos by the interruptions we encounter. Instead, we will measure them by our priorities and let God speak to us through them. The power of God living through us will also provide balance in our lives. We will no longer find ourselves moving from one extreme to another; we will let God be central in all that we do.

The power of God does not have to be a fantasy or something we believe is a thing of the past. God's power is real. It is so real that we can live the Christian life, even in the midst of the distractions, interruptions, and pressures of our times. The key is for us to continually reconnect with God.